AZURE ANGELOV >> DEIDRE PET
University of Indianapolis   *University of Indic*

EDUCATIONAL
MARKETING

>> MORE THAN JUST TELLING **YOUR** STORY

Kendall Hunt
publishing company

Cover image © Shutterstock, Inc.

www.kendallhunt.com
Send all inquiries to:
4050 Westmark Drive
Dubuque, IA 52004-1840

Copyright © 2015 by Azure Angelov, Deidre Pettinga, and David Bateman

ISBN 978-1-4652-7492-2

Printed in the United States of America

CONTENTS

INTRODUCTION

From 1998 to 2004, the US Postal Service sponsored a professional cycling team. Many questioned the need for a federal agency to engage in marketing of any form. Here is an example of a complaint:

> federally-affiliated anything is likely so because the goods/services produced tend to serve a basic/commodity need . . . marketing . . . seems unnecessary. (ChicagoNow, 2013).

However, at about the same time the US Postal Service had been losing market share, a trend that has continued (United States Postal Service, 2012). A US Post Office is unique in that no other place brings all of society together in the same way, and it seems hard to believe that an institution so central to American social and political life is losing cultural market share at roughly the same pace as newspapers and bookstores (Gelfand, 2012). The US Postal Service does much more than just deliver mail:

> Letter carriers serve as a kind of neighborhood watch; that postal workers help reestablish contact with citizens after natural disasters like Hurricane Katrina; and that the postal service plays a role in government services such as voter registration and census completion. (Wildlife officials in many Midwestern states, including Ohio, still rely on rural mail carrier surveys to estimate populations of everything from rabbits to quail.) Most strikingly, it pointed out the role that the Postal Service plays in nurturing social links, fostering civic pride, and "promoting community identity through local post offices and services that support civic engagement" (Gelfand, 2012).

US public schools are facing a similar decline. With competition from the various school choice options, the percentage of students attending public schools is dropping very quickly. But we need to realize that public schools, like the example above of the multifaceted US Postal Service, are more than just places for students to receive an education, they are the backbone of a community. They are a place for voting; a place for meeting; a place for Friday night football; the provider of educational services for the vast majority of the residents; a provider of breakfasts and lunches for less affluent children; a major stable employer of the community; the identity of the community. But this is changing. Like the US Postal Service, that once held a virtual monopoly on the services they provided, public schools are losing market share, and with it many communities will be losing all the many important elements a public school provides.

A typical response from public school employees regarding marketing is viewing this as simply the need to tell their story. However, that is communication and, while communication is an extremely important part of the marketing function, it is just a part of a bigger picture. Organizations that attempt to whittle the marketing function down solely to communication risk enormous failures. History is full of case studies where this has happened.

Consider, for example, Oldsmobile's attempt in the late 1980s to broaden its target audience to include younger car buyers. The carmaker's research identified that the majority of new car buyers were in the 20–30 age segment. However, most of those people viewed Oldsmobile as a brand for older people. To reach out to the younger buyers, Oldsmobile's advertising agency, Leo Burnett, developed what became a wildly successful ad campaign with the tag line, jingle, and television ads that featured the young adult children of well-recognized celebrities, such as Ringo Starr, Leonard Nimoy, William Shatner, and Harry Belafonte, among others. The popular ads brought young car buyers into Oldsmobile dealerships in droves to see the vehicle that was featured in the ads. Unfortunately, what they found was a product that had very few of the features they wanted and a price tag that was well above what they were able to afford. Although the ad campaign was deemed wildly popular with consumers, many business critics point to the overall marketing effort as the beginning of the end for Oldsmobile. The mishap highlights the notion that telling a good story is not enough. It showcases the simple truth: marketing is much more than communication.

Historically, public school systems in the United States have had a virtual monopoly on the provision of educational services across the country. Educators never had to worry about getting new students—they always had a steady supply. However, times have changed. Due to declining resources for public schools, changing demographics, vouchers, and heightened scrutiny over test scores—coupled with an explosion in the number of alternative and private schools—public schools in the US are facing uncharted waters. They are, in many ways, completely unprepared for an evolution that has been forced upon them.

With this changing educational landscape, public perception of public schools is dismal in many areas. Newspapers often focus their coverage of public schools on low test scores, crimes at schools, accidents on school buses, demands for better (or more) teacher pay, and the occasional need to talk about raising taxes to pay for schools generally characterized as mismanaged. The only good news a public school might get is a description of the success of a sports team, though that is often left to the whims of the sports editor of the local paper.

Public schools do many good things and play a vital role in our society. Unfortunately, people don't seem to know this part of the story. Public schools tend to have wider courses of study, more qualified teachers, guidance services, transportation, more extracurricular activities, social services, special education services and—due to their larger sizes—they often offer the students a richer experience which helps prepare them for life. In spite of this, public school employees have tremendous difficulty making the local community aware of the good things happening in their public schools—all the while recognizing it is the positive facets of the public school system that help distinguish it in the face of growing competition. However, just knowing the story isn't enough. Public school employees are not helpless victims of today's education policies; they are in fact, the valiant defenders of the future of public education. While it has not been a skill set traditionally or explicitly taught, public school employees must become masters of their own destiny. Today's public school employees need to understand why, when, where, and how to market their schools to continue to serve our communities in this changing educational climate.

One of the biggest shifts in thinking that must take place is for public school employees to begin to see that in today's society there is competition for students, and therefore there is a need to think about how to market their school. To market their school, public school employees are going to have to understand what they do well, understand what the others have to offer, and change their thinking about getting information out to others. This ideological shift is a difficult one to make and can initially leave passionate educators feeling defeated. If public schools are going to thrive in today's society it is necessary to recognize and respond to the current field of education. It is professionally naive to sit idly by and wish for the good old days or maintain the status quo, rather than evolving to the reality while working toward the future educators believe possible.

One of the most important factors in marketing a school, or any product, for that matter, is understanding the customer. Due to the changing competitive landscape in education, it is becoming vital to understand how families select schools for their children. No longer is it just enrolling the child in the closest school and hope all goes well. Families today are shopping for schools in a manner similar to the way they research a new appliance or automobile prior to purchase. Unfortunately, many public schools are unprepared to assist families in this decision-making process. Public schools need new tools to navigate the changing dynamics of education. They need to engage with families and their communities when developing new programs or choosing which programs to close, understand the reasons for telling others about what they do, and then work, using new media and old, to develop a comprehensive and coherent strategy for successfully marketing their program. That is the purpose of this book.

A school principal can't just tell a secretary to put out a press release to the local paper. A superintendent can no longer simply ask a district level communications specialist to communicate all of the good things going on. Much more is expected, and it needs to be part of a unified plan. The lines between marketing and public relations have blurred for public schools and what may have worked in the past may not be the best now. The most obvious route may also not help achieve the ultimate goal; helping to successfully market a school or program

This innovative book, *Educational Marketing: More Than Just Telling Your Story*, provides public school employees clear and concise strategies to develop their marketing skill set and solve daily problems facing public schools across the country. The authors come from a public school background and a marketing background, and understand the complexity of needs facing public schools that have to do more with less. While there are numerous business-book models on how to market a product, this book is unique in that it describes effective strategies and techniques for specifically marketing public education to the community. There is really nothing like it out there—a book written jointly by educators and a marketer serving as a primer on marketing a school. Families, school boards, community members, and policy makers need a balanced understanding to draw from when making decisions about public schools. In order for this to happen, public educators must become more savvy and strategic at marketing their programs in this complex competitive environment.

Today's administrators need to understand why, when, where, and how to market their schools to continue to serve their communities in this changing educational climate. One of the biggest shifts in thinking that must take place is for educators to begin to see that, in today's society, there is competition for students. This competitive environment calls for educators to appreciate the need to market their school. To be successful in this endeavor, public school educators have to understand what they do well, what their communities want from them, identify what their competitors have to offer, and, most importantly, change their beliefs that marketing and communication are synonymous. If public schools are going to thrive in today's competitive environment, they must recognize and respond to current market conditions.

References

ChicagoNow. (2013). Why did the USPS sponsor Lance Armstrong anyway? Retrieved from http://www.chicagonow.com/cinnamon-twists/2013/04/why-did-the-usps-sponsor-lance-armstrong-anyway/

Gelfand, A. (2012). Bye, bye, USPS? Denison Magazine. Retrieved from http://denisonmagazine.com/2012/features/bye-bye-usps/

United State Postal Service. (2012). Plan to profitability: Five year business plan, February 16, 2012. Retrieved from http://about.usps.com/news/national-releases/2012/pr12_0217profitability.pdf

ABOUT THE AUTHORS

L-R: Pettinga, Bateman, Angelov.
Photo Courtesy of Kelsey Bess, Eight 31 Photography.

Azure D. S. Angelov

Dr. Angelov has a BA in Elementary and Special Education from Marian University, an MS in Effective Teaching from Butler University, and a PhD in Special Education and Multicultural Education from Indiana University. In addition to being a special education teacher, publishing research, and sitting on state and national committees, she has also helped several schools in developing countries establish programs for students with exceptionalities. Dr. Angelov has received the YWCA's Woman of Achievement award, the Association of Independent Liberal Arts Colleges for Teacher Education Scholar Award, Marian University's Outstanding Young Alumni award, the Indiana Council for Exceptional Children's Outstanding Child Advocate award, and the Metropolitan School District of Wayne Township's M.G. Raby Distinguished Service Award. Currently, Dr. Angelov is an Associate Professor and Chair of the Institutional Review Board at the University of Indianapolis and a special education evaluator for the Indianapolis Mayor's Office of Education Innovation.

Deidre M. Pettinga

Dr. Pettinga is an Assistant Professor of Marketing at the University of Indianapolis, School of Business. She earned a BS in Public and Corporate Communication and MBA from Butler University, Indianapolis, IN, as well as an MA in Psychology and a PhD in Media Psychology from Fielding Graduate University, Santa Barbara, CA. Prior to joining the faculty at the University of Indianapolis, she worked for 20 years in advertising and marketing. She has presented to numerous business, civic, and education organizations, including the Indiana Center for Family, School & Community Partnerships, the Marketing Management Association, and the American Camp Association. Her articles have appeared in the Journal of Academic Administration in Higher Education, Journal of the Academy of Business Education, and the International Journal of Motorsport Management. Currently, Dr. Pettinga teaches marketing coursework for Business majors and marketing and communications coursework for the MBA in Educational Leadership program.

David Bateman

Dr. Bateman has a BA in Government and Foreign Affairs from the University of Virginia, an MEd in Special Education from William and Mary, and a PhD in Special Education from the University of Kansas. He has been a classroom teacher of students with learning disabilities, behavior disorders, intellectual disabilities, and hearing impairments. He is a professor of special education at Shippensburg University of Pennsylvania where he teaches courses to future teachers and administrators in learning disabilities, special education law, and the introduction to special education. He is former Due Process Hearing Officer for the Commonwealth of Pennsylvania and is Past-President of the Pennsylvania Federation Council for Exceptional Children. His latest area of research has been on preventing litigation in special education. He is currently Public Policy Chair of the Division for Learning Disabilities and is active in the Consortium for Citizens with Disabilities in Washington, DC.

CHAPTER 1

The Value Exchange: Building Relationships With Educational Consumers

Marketing takes a day to learn. Unfortunately, it takes a lifetime to master.

—*Philip Kotler, Professor at the Kellogg School of Management, Northwestern University.*

Google "schools." Better yet, Google "good schools." The results you will come up with will likely include a K–12 online schools, DeVry Tech, virtual schools, best high schools under US News and World Report, and a guide for choosing schools in the UK that have embedded advertisement for K–12 online schools. You would be very unlikely to find your school (if you were to find your school it would likely be due to a sports score). Now, if you Google "great schools," you will find GreatSchools.org and find your school compared to others around you with each of you given a rating based on a variety of quantifiable indicators (data).

Parents are now searching for schools in ways unheard of 10 or 20 years ago and there is a competitive marketplace for education that public school employees are completely unprepared for. The initial response is to put out a press release extolling the latest test scores hoping it will be placed in the local newspaper. Even if that does get published, who reads it? What does it really say about your school? Are decision makers paying attention to that story? Are parents? Does it really level the playing field with all information available from other schools?

Many public school administrators and teachers think marketing is sending out a press release. Does a single press release market your school? Do businesses send out a single press release to market their school? This book is about marketing for public school employees—not how to compose a press release.

Lena Pan/Shutterstock.com

What Does This Mean for Public School Employees?

For many educators, discussing education as a product and the landscape of public education as a marketplace is an ideological shift. While much of the debate about school choice and competition has focused on the positives and negatives of these types of educational systems, this book takes a different perspective. This book is not supporting or combating competition or choice movements. It does, however, recognize public schools currently functioning within a competitive environment. This book is meant to serve as a tool for public educators to navigate competitive waters. The marketing of education is not negative, and is not in contrast to the overall mission of public education. A more specific understanding of the role marketing plays in public education is a vital next step for educators in their pursuit of innovation and evolution. To move forward, public educators must embrace a proactive role in deliberately sharing the importance of what is provided to students and communities, while recognizing many others in town offer similar services.

Public education in the US started in the 1800s. It was originally established as part of the Department of War when it became apparent the country could not sustain an effective military with large numbers of illiterate soldiers (Cross, 2010). Over the years public education grew in size and mission, reflecting the changes of the nation. Since its creation, public education has served a variety of purposes for our society. For decades, public education has produced citizens who make informed decisions when voting. For many Americans, it was the opportunity for a free public education that provided them the tools they needed to change their lives. Public education has produced students with the will and drive to become whatever their hearts and minds choose. Public education has produced generations of taxpayers who are able to provide for themselves and others. The true impact of our product, a free public education, is virtually immeasurable. For public schools to truly move forward, public school employees must recognize it is their obligation to learn how to be masters of their own destiny and share their work in a way that educates others of the value of a public education. As public schools find themselves yet again facing the expectations of an evolving society, it is important to recognize it is not the only profession that has needed to embrace marketing as a means to grow.

Several other public entities have embraced the importance of marketing strategies as competition entered their fields. In 1973, the Department of Defense became an all-volunteer organization and began its first marketing campaign to educate the public on their services and opportunities (Cross, 2010). These efforts still continue today and offer the public an alternative understanding of the military experience from those portrayed by popular media. In the face of technological advances and competitive markets, public libraries have also turned to marketing strategies to continue to pursue their mission (Robinson, 2012). For public libraries, they have determined that to thrive they must make sure the public understands what they provide and center their efforts on being more user focused. One of the most notable public entities that have strong ties with marketing campaigns is the US Postal Service. In the age of the Internet and e-mail, the US Postal Service recognized a disconnect between the way customers saw mail and utilized large-scale marketing campaigns to inform the public of their services (Schuyler, 2001). As each of these entities began to move forward, one of the first steps was for them to recognize how what was expected of them has changed.

As public schools look to the future, they must recognize the changes in the societal landscape and decide what this means. Private schools in the US began in the sixteenth century as missionary entities. Many private schools across the country have maintained these religious roots and their own identities outside of public forums, leaving a very dichotomous existence between the two. The lines between public and private education were very clear and bureaucratic systems were in place based on these boundaries. The recent legislative push for choice and competition has muddied these once clear waters. Public education is now one piece of a much larger and more complex educational marketplace. As the marketplace has changed, so must the behaviors of public schools.

The field of educational research has spent a considerable amount of energy examining the relationship between schools and families. Much of this research has focused on understanding what schools can do to partner with families to support the academic achievement of their students. In this new era of choice and competition, understanding and building relationships with families is only part of the story. Public schools now need to know why families choose their school, why they stay, and why they leave. From a marketing perspective, we must begin to examine the relationship between the public school and the community through the lens of the value exchange model. This perspective allows public schools a more holistic view of the relationship they engage in with the community, as well as the services they provide communities and families in exchange for their tax dollars.

Public schools have been rightfully focused on the product they provide. Many conversations are about test scores and other singular measures of success of schools. This post-Industrial Revolution era perspective on marketing is known as a product concept of marketing. Public educators have been focused on sharing only one aspect of the services they provide, many times in a reactionary fashion. To thrive in the educational marketplace of today, public education must begin to engage with a societal concept of marketing. To begin our understanding of public school marketing, it is important to understand what marketing is and how it has evolved.

As is the case in a variety of industries today, educators are being pulled in a number of directions. Trite as it may sound, they are being challenged to wear a number of different hats and, in general, accomplish more with less. The changing landscape has forced administrators and teachers to understand concepts related to business and marketing, which are generally outside the scope of their academic background and professional expertise. Schools today are being asked to market themselves but are not given the instruction on what it means to market a school, let alone the resources to do it properly. Most people think they have a general understanding of what marketing is all about because, as consumers, we've been exposed to a wide variety of marketing communications efforts in the form of advertisements, sales pitches, and other promotional activities. However, marketing communications is just a subset of marketing, a discipline encompassing far more than the act of producing an ad or sponsoring an event.

The development of Marketing as a discipline has been an outgrowth of how business has evolved over the past 150 years. In the post-Industrial Revolution era, business management has changed its philosophy a number of different times on how to sell a product to a customer (Armstrong & Kotler, 2013; Kotler, 1988). In early industrial times, management tended to operate under the Production Concept, believing consumers would buy goods that are readily available and highly affordable. As a result, the focus of the operation was on producing goods at such a level needed to realize economies of scale, thereby making the goods both available and affordable. This concept is operationally successful as long as demand exceeds supply. However, as competition grew and a number of different organizations were able to produce and sell similar goods at affordable prices, business managers shifted their thinking to what is known as the Product Concept. While this philosophy still emphasizes mass production, it states consumers will favor the superior good; therefore, emphasis should be placed on continually improving the product to gain a competitive advantage.

By the early 1900s there were a number of businesses producing goods—leading to excess supply. This was coupled by an economic recession, causing a decrease in demand. With inventories piling up, management philosophy changed yet again, resulting in the Selling Concept, which holds consumers will not buy goods unless the firm undertakes a large-scale selling and promotional effort. It was in this period the traveling salesman was born (Solomon, 2004). However, none of the managerial concepts to date placed much emphasis on the consumer. Designing, producing, and selling products were more important. It wasn't until the post-World War II era that companies started to think about the consumer. The era of the Marketing Concept ushered in a focus on understanding the needs of the customer. This philosophy holds that only by satisfying the needs and wants of the consumer will an organization be successful. The Marketing Concept is still practiced today, though it has evolved to

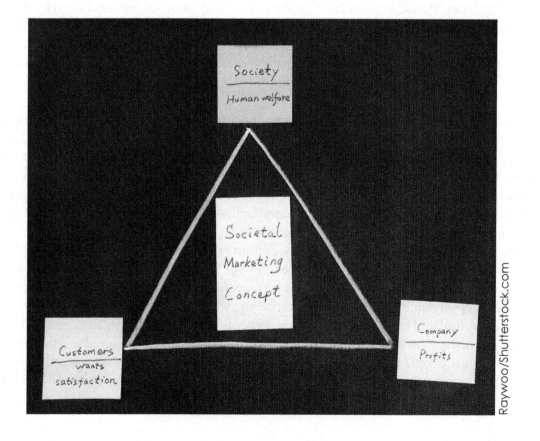

some extent to what is referred to as the Holistic or Societal Marketing Concept, which still stresses the importance of meeting consumers' needs, but doing it in such a way to benefit not only the consumer but society as well. Green Marketing and Sustainable Marketing practices are examples of the Societal Marketing Concept.

Along with the evolution of business management philosophies, the definition of marketing has also changed over time. The American Marketing Association (AMA) is credited with developing the first official definition of marketing back in 1938, after the US Census Bureau requested the Association's help in providing a consistent definition of marketing to be used by all government agencies (Armstrong & Kotler, 2013; Smith, 1956). While there are numerous ways individuals and organizations define marketing, most commonly accepted definitions of marketing include the following verbiage:

> Marketing is the set of commercial processes involved in developing and maintaining relationships with consumers for the purpose of delivering value in order to capture value in return.

Central to this definition is the notion of the value exchange. In other words, businesses aren't merely producing goods and selling them to people. Rather, they are giving up something of value (the good) in exchange for something else of value (money, in most cases). Viewed in this light, we can begin to understand the importance of consumers to the equation. Buyers are not simply getting something from the seller; they are giving up something to get something in return. In most cases what they give up is, in fact, money, though that isn't always the case. For example, if a person makes a donation of a pint of blood to a blood bank, one might think there is no exchange. Although the blood bank receives the donated blood, the consumer does, in fact, get something back: a sense of good will or satisfaction for having done something worthwhile, not to mention a cookie and a glass of orange juice! The two parties have exchanged something of value.

We can begin to think of marketing as an exchange that occurs between the buyer and the seller, shown in the model below.

As the Marketing Model illustrates, the two parties come together to trade items of worth or significance. For the Seller, the item produced doesn't always have to be a good or service—like a pair of shoes or a haircut. As demonstrated in the blood bank example, the value blood banks provide consumers has nothing to do with any manufactured item. The marketers at the American Red Cross,

FIGURE 1.1—The Marketing Model

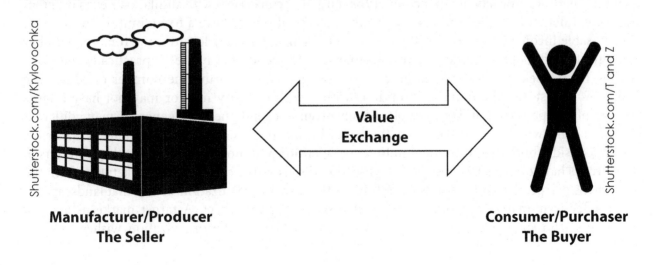

Manufacturer/Producer
The Seller

Value Exchange

Consumer/Purchaser
The Buyer

Shutterstock.com/Krylovochka

Shutterstock.com/T and Z

for example, focus on the benefits of giving blood with how good it feels to donate, and that it will help ensure there is enough blood available for people in need (American Red Cross, 2013). Likewise for the Buyer, the thing that is given up isn't always measured in terms of money. It can be a donation of time or blood or even a vote for a particular political candidate. People cast their vote with the hope that it will result in the kind of representation they want in a particular public office. Value exchanges can exist on many levels and they are at the root of Marketing.

With this in mind, we offer a more streamlined definition of Marketing, one centered on the concept of the value exchange. We believe Marketing can be defined as "All those activities that facilitate the exchange of value between the buyer and the seller." As we will discuss in Chapter Three, the "activities" facilitating the value exchange can be broken out into four areas: Product, Price, Place, and Promotion or the Marketing Mix. These are generally referred to as the 4 P's. Other sources have suggested the inclusion of additional "P's"—such as People, Processes, Philosophy, and a variety of others. However, for the discussion of public school marketing, we will confine our definition to include the traditional 4 P's. While the marketing model and definition are admittedly simple at this point, throughout the book we will layer in additional concepts that will help broaden the reader's understanding of Marketing.

Finally, it should be stressed that although the Marketing Model showcases one Seller and one Buyer, in reality, there are multiple Buyers and Sellers. In nearly every aspect of their purchasing lives, consumers have a variety of options available to them. Likewise, Sellers do not simply produce and sell a single good to one customer. If that were the case, it would be quite simple for a business to understand what a purchaser wants and customize a solution for that particular individual. Today, most goods are mass-produced for a large audience—a collection of consumers who have a lot of competitors vying for their attention and money. The rare exception to the competitive environment is found in the case of a monopoly, such as an electric utility. To some extent, public school systems have had, until recently, territorial monopolies. Good school systems in the right part of town continually flourished because people wanted to buy a house in that area so their children could go to the schools in that district. However, the environment has shifted. Traditional public schools have found themselves in an increasingly competitive arena with charter schools, vouchers, private schools, online education, and inter-district choice programs becoming more widespread.

Positioning

As noted above, the marketing relationship between the Seller and the Buyer does not happen in a vacuum. There are a variety of other competitors targeting consumers with similar—or even different offers. By different offers, we must recognize that nearly all Buyers have a fixed limit on the amount of disposable income they can or will spend on a certain activity, say leisure-time fun. The number of leisure-time fun opportunities where consumers could spend their money is practically endless—ranging from weekend getaways, to movies, to bowling, and so forth. The number of competing categories is vast and the number of options within each category may or may not have a large number of competitors in it. For example, on any given weekend, there are generally many different movies playing, whereas in a small town, there may be only one bowling alley. The point is marketers need to consider both their direct and indirect competition and monitor the impact that both sets of competitors have on their business. The next section discusses the competitive marketplace from the consumer's perspective and how to successfully distinguish an organization within that landscape.

To effectively market a product, one must first identify the target. A target market is a set of consumers who share a common need or other characteristics the organization wishes to serve

(Armstrong & Kotler, 2013). The common need or characteristic used to identify a market segment can be based on a number of variables. These include geographic, demographic, psychographic, and behavioral (Kotler, 1988). Geographic area can include regions of the country, urban versus rural areas, or even particular climates. Demographic variables consist of age, sex, family size, income, occupation, education, religion, ability, race, and nationality. Psychographic variables combine psychological, sociological, and anthropological characteristics, such as social class, lifestyle (such as outdoorsmen or scrap-bookers), or personality (such as ambitious or frugal) (Solomon, 2004). Behavioral variables an organization may want to consider as a basis for market segmentation include purchase occasions (such as holidays or anniversaries), user status (such as potential user, current user, ex-user), usage rate (such as heavy or light user), and attitude toward the product (ranging from enthusiastic to hostile). An organization should identify which segments exist and then select the one or ones they believe are the most viable. A viable market segment is one with measurable purchasing power, is large enough to remain profitable, can be readily accessed and served by the organization, and will actively respond to the marketing effort.

Once a segment is selected, there are three basic options to target the segment: very broadly (undifferentiated marketing), very narrowly (niche or micromarketing), or somewhere in the middle (differentiated or concentrated marketing) (Smith, 1956). An undifferentiated marketing effort is one in which the organization ignores any differences that may exist among segments and targets the entire market with one offer. The Marketing Mix strategy targets everyone. Examples range from basic food staples to postage stamps; the product and the way it is marketed to people is all the same.

At the other end of the spectrum is niche or micromarketing. Here, the organization identifies a small segment not currently being served by other competitors. This could be a local marketing effort or even individualized or custom marketing. This is more common in professional services marketing, such as architecture or legal services where "product" solutions and even the marketing messages are tailored specifically to each individual client. However, in the business-to-consumer realm, an example can be found in real estate sales, where sales representatives customize a set of homes to show to clients based on their individual needs and preferences. Where schools are concerned, examples of niches include charter or private schools targeting specific student populations, like students with exceptional needs.

Differentiated or concentrated marketing falls in-between undifferentiated and niche marketing. Here, organizations serve multiple segments, each with a specific Marketing Mix of product, price, place, and promotion. An example includes Hilton Hotels, whose portfolio of brands includes, among others, the luxury Conrad Hilton Hotels, Hilton Garden Inn with more of a residential atmosphere for business travelers, and the mid-level, value-priced Hampton Inn (Hilton Worldwide, 2013). The product offerings are designed to serve different segments and the price points vary. In addition, the placement of a Conrad Hilton Hotel is more likely to be either in the heart of a large metropolitan area or at a destination location, such as an island resort. Conversely, a Hampton Inn is more readily situated off an interstate exchange. Finally, the strategies used to promote each brand use different messaging and media strategies. The Hampton Inn, which targets a larger traveling segment, such as middle-class families, is more likely to advertise on the mass medium of television than the Conrad brand. As can be seen from these examples, the Marketing Mix used is a function of the target segment the organization wishes to serve.

At least from a product perspective, most traditional public schools could be characterized as falling within the Differentiated segment strategy. Naturally, school systems target children by age—with elementary, middle, and high schools. However, additional programs target specific populations; examples include vocational training, special education, as well as GED and International Baccalaureate programs, among others.

Beyond identifying a segment to serve and selecting a targeting strategy, the organization must select a value proposition, which helps distinguish the brand from the competition (Armstrong & Kotler, 2013). The value proposition also helps consumers identify the value of the potential exchange. In other words, by knowing the value of the product or service, Buyers can decide the level of value they would need to exchange to obtain it. To organize the variety of options available in any one category, consumers use mental cues to help them distinguish one product from another. Recognizing this, marketers must develop a positioning strategy to help influence consumers' understanding of the product's value proposition (Solomon, 2004). Positioning allows the organization to design the brand's image and value proposition so the buyers in the target segment appreciate the distinguishing features of the brand, relative to the competition. For any one category, an organization can research consumers' perceptions of competitors based on key distinguishing factors, such as customer service or luxury, by using a perceptual map. The figure below shows an example of how consumers might evaluate a series of fictitious women's fragrances based on key variables of Price (plotted on the Y-axis) and Image (plotted on the X-axis).

Generally speaking, a product can distinguish itself in two ways: price and differentiation (Porter, 1980). Competitors seeking to engage in price competition are typically larger organizations with considerable market share who are able to enjoy the kind of economies of scale resulting in lower production and operating costs. Organizations operating under these conditions are generally able to charge a lower price and are in a better position to compete effectively when additional competitors wage price wars against them. It should be recognized the price and cost-structure model that exists within the public schools category is unique. These distinctive characteristics will be discussed in greater detail in Chapter Six, *Price*.

Beyond price, a brand can also position itself based on a unique differentiating characteristic, such as customer service, styling, or performance. Results of perceptual mapping research can assist marketers with establishing an effective positioning strategy. As Ries and Trout argued, positioning allows marketers to establish a stake-hold or frame of reference in the mind of the consumer (Ries & Trout, 1982). An effectively established and articulately communicated position strategy needs to be rooted in a positioning statement. A positioning statement summarizes the brand's positioning by identifying the target segment and its need, the brand concept, and the point of difference (Caler & Reagan, 2001). Below are several examples of product positioning statements:

FIGURE 1.2—Fragrance Perceptual Map

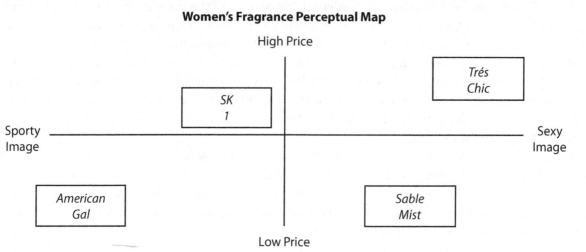

Zip-Car: To urban-dwelling, educated techno-savvy consumers [target], when you use Zipcar car-sharing service instead of owning a car [brand concept], you save money while reducing your carbon footprint [points of difference] (Republished with permission of John Wiley, from Kellogg on Marketing, The Kellogg School of Marketing, 2nd Edition, 2010; permission conveyed through Copyright Clearance Center, Inc).

For example, an up-scale, suburban health club that offers personal training, spa, and other fitness-related services may position itself thusly.

To discerning adults determined to remain healthy and fit [target], our fitness center is a full-service, personalized training facility [brand concept] that provides you with individualized training sessions, nutritional counseling, and spa services in a professional and selective environment, to help you meet your fitness goals and maintain your healthy profile [points of difference].

It should be noted a positioning statement should not be confused with a mission statement. A mission statement or statement of purpose details the organization's purpose or reason for existence. Positioning statements identify a product's membership within a particular category and distinguish the unique characteristics of the product, which differentiate it from other competing brands found in the same category. For example, global consumer products giant Procter & Gamble utilizes the following Statement of Purpose:

We will provide branded products and services of superior quality and value that improve the lives of the world's consumers, now and for generations to come. As a result, consumers will reward us with leadership sales, profit and value creation, allowing our people, our shareholders and the communities in which we live and work to prosper (Copyright © 2013 Procter & Gamble. Reprinted by permission).

However, the company's website details the 50 brands the company produces and distributes. In terms of the target segment being served, the product concept, and the points of difference, the Pampers brand, is positioned quite differently from Cover Girl or Head & Shoulders. Organizations need mission statements as well as positioning statements.

Many schools develop mission statements such as:

For elementary schools:
- Our school seeks to create a challenging learning environment encouraging high expectations for success through development-appropriate instruction that allows for individual differences and learning styles.
- Our school believes learning is maximized when it takes place in an environment enriched with support, encouragement and assistance.
- Our school ensures every student's intellectual and emotional growth and to promote effective citizenship.

For a middle school:
- Our school's mission is to provide students with the skills and exploratory experiences that enable them to reach their fullest potential as independent thinkers.

For a high school:
- Our school strives to be a community of learners in which all members use their minds well and care about one another.

As you can see, these mission statements are clearly different from a positioning statement. As will be discussed further in this book, the product's positioning should serve as a guiding frame of reference for all decisions related to the Marketing Mix. For example, take the format of a positioning statement; it's quite straightforward. It doesn't read or sound like a jingle or commercial slogan. Nonetheless, the positioning statement can (and should) be used to guide the development of an appropriate commercial message. Several years ago, a shipping company featured an advertising slogan that made reference to a "tight ship." This cleverly-worded parody effectively captured the company's positioning of superior logistics capabilities. Managers should continually refer to the positioning statement to ensure all aspects of the Marketing Mix uphold the product's positioning—beginning with the product. Therefore, organizations need to make sure that the product or service they are delivering to consumers actually *delivers* on the value proposition.

What Do Outsiders "Know" About Your School?

Most of the research and dialogue about the relationship between families and public schools has focused on partnerships between the two groups with intentions of improving the academic performance of students (Henderson, Map, Johnson, & Davies, 2007). In some cases, this research also discusses the role public schools can play in communities and notes the importance of teachers living within the communities they serve (Murrell, 2001). The crux of much of this work focuses on the personal relationships and interactions between educators and families. As public educators think about their relationship with families and the larger community, they must also understand they are funded by tax dollars and essentially work for taxpayers. Public schools provide a public service to the larger community, as well as to individual families. From a marketing perspective, it is important for public schools to identify and understand the viable market segment they serve.

Previously, public schools have had a certain group of students they served based on geographic location. In many ways, public schools held the lion's share of power in their relationships with families because they were the only option for many families. In a competitive market, this is no longer the case. Families that previously had very few options are now bombarded with many choices. Research has shown schools often offer services and programs for families based on what they believe families need, rather than by collecting data from families to find out what they want (Smiley, Howland, & Anderson, 2008). Working from inaccurate assumptions about a community often leads to low levels of family participation and tensions between schools and families. Public schools must begin to analyze data about the communities they serve as closely as they analyze data on student achievement. In a landscape of choice, identifying the families to be served and their expectations of public schools is important. Public schools must begin to focus on the families in their community that utilize or will utilize public education options in their communities.

Once families are identified that will most likely choose a public school option for their children, it is important to collect data on how they perceive the school.

Here are some questions that will help:

1. What is the reputation of the public school in the community?
2. When families describe their experience with the school to their neighbors, what do they say?
3. What do realtors tell potential homebuyers in the community about the school?
4. What do pediatricians tell their patients about the public school?
5. What type of media coverage has the public school received in the last several years?
6. How do the alumni describe their experience with the school?
7. What do employers, other schools, or colleges say about the graduates?
8. After collecting these types of data, educators must begin to decipher the validity of these perceptions. Are they the perceptions one wants families and communities to have about the school?
9. Are there any perceptions that are surprises?

Not all of the questions are important, but each will assess the viable market segment and perceptions of the school, and understanding of the competition. Public schools have a long history of working with the private schools within their jurisdictions. In many capacities, public and private schools have worked together to serve their communities. Both entities have provided a necessary service and the relationship between both types of schools were fairly clear-cut. Each type of school served a different student population within their community, so competition was of little concern. Now that various types of publicly funded schools are competing for the same students, it is important to identify the public school options families have in the jurisdiction.

Here are some questions that will help with the identification:

1. Which public schools in the area are targeting the same families?
2. Once the competition is identified, it is important to begin to develop an understanding of what they offer families. Why do families choose those schools?
3. Why do they stay in those schools?
4. Why do they leave those schools?
5. How do families and the community perceive those schools?
6. What type of media coverage have those schools received in the last few years?
7. How do alumni describe their experience with that school?
8. What do employers, other schools, or colleges say about their graduates?

After collecting perception data on the school and the competition, one can begin to understand the competitive landscape. At this point there needs to begin the development of an appropriate marketing mix for the targeted market segment. It is helpful to develop a value proposition grid based on the public perception of the school and the competition. Plot the school and the competition schools on the map. Figure 1.3 shows an example of how educational consumers might evaluate competitor schools based on Extracurricular Options (plotted on the Y-axis) and Academic Achievement (plotted on the X-axis).

By distinguishing the school from its competitors in this manner, one can develop a positioning statement aligning with the mission statement. Keep in mind the positioning statement is a frame of reference for the families and community. Additionally, the positioning strategy should be deeply rooted in the positioning statement. It must convey to the target market segment both brand concept and points differentiating the school from the competition. Below are a few examples of public school positioning statements:

West Side High School: To highly educated, sport-savvy families [target], when you choose to send your child to West Side High School instead of a charter [brand concept], you provide your child with an academically rigorous and athletically competitive experience [points of difference].

East Grove Charter School: To academically focused families who want their children to focus on intellectual pursuits [target], an East Grove education provides academic experiences and consultants [brand concept] that offer your student a superior foundation in academics and an easier transition into a prestigious university [points of difference].

Both of these examples can work in tandem with the mission statement of the school and as part of the strategic plan. A positioning statement allows educators to synthesize their perceptual data in a meaningful way for families as they make educational choices. The importance for public schools to begin to tell their own stories cannot be overstated. Recently, public education has been the subject of popular media, Hollywood movies, and legislative efforts. Public education has ample opportunity to grow in their efforts to strategically tell their own story and offer an alternate view from those offered by various media outlets. The focus of local and national news outlets is to provide quick snapshots of

FIGURE 1.3—Public School Perceptual Map

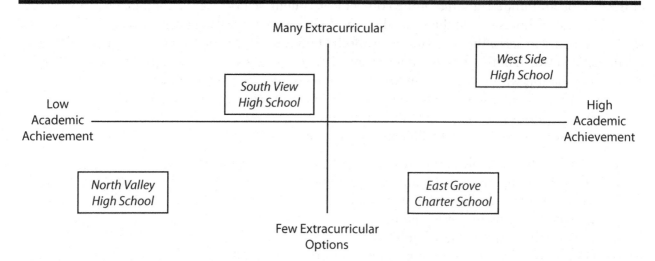

newsworthy events within their community. Mainstream movies are meant to entertain and generate profits. Neither of these entities is meant to tell the story of public education. Educators have allowed these entities too much power in shaping public opinion about the service they provide communities. By being proactive, outspoken, thoughtful, and strategic about sharing the benefits of public education to the larger communities, educators can begin to offer a more informed and authentic perspective.

Chapter 1—SPOTLIGHT: Indianapolis Public Schools

When Dr. Lewis Ferebee assumed the role of Superintendent of Indiana's largest school system, Indianapolis Public Schools (IPS), he entered a district that was operating at a $30 million deficit, where more than half of the schools were failing, and enrollment was declining—dropping from its glory days of serving 100,000+ students to an enrollment of 30,000. Undaunted by the statistics, the superintendent quickly recognized these were not problems that could be overcome with a simple press release or media blitz.

In a series of radio and TV interviews with local media, the Superintendent acknowledged that IPS is operating in a saturated educational climate and that his job is to look at the population the district is serving and design alternative programs that meet the needs of the students and families. Not just the magnet programs but all programs.

In his 100-day Entry plan, Dr. Ferebee outlined five goals:

► Gather information carefully about the organization and community;
► Establish a strong community presence early;
► Assess the state of the school district while gaining historical perspective;
► Identify critical challenges and opportunities;
► Build on strengths by creating a supportive network of critical friends to the district and leveraging resources that will help advance Indianapolis Public Schools.

ENTRY PLAN CONCLUSION

Lewis D. Ferebee, Ed.D.
Indianapolis Public Schools

June 24, 2014

*my*IPS

executive summary and introduction

Upon transitioning to Indianapolis Public Schools (IPS) in September 2013 as Superintendent, I developed an entry plan to guide my efforts over my first 100 days. Released during my first week on the job, this plan provided a foundation for assessing the district's strengths and opportunities, identifying areas needing immediate focus and those requiring long-range planning.

The plan included five overarching goals, five objectives and initial entry actions that I would pursue within 100 days. The five overarching goals would enable me to

1) gather information carefully about the organization and community;

2) establish a strong community presence early;

3) assess the state of the school district while gaining historical perspective;

4) identify critical challenges and opportunities; and

5) build on strengths by creating a supportive network of critical friends to the district and leveraging resources that would help advance Indianapolis Public Schools.

These overarching goals supported the development of five broad objectives to prioritize the work of our core leadership team.

I have benefitted from thoughtful and diverse experiences that assist me in gaining a comprehensive understanding of the school district and the greater Indianapolis community.

I have enjoyed engaging students, faculty, staff, core leadership, parents, community stakeholders and community leaders. I have reviewed pertinent documents, financial reports and student achievement data. Another major component of my transition efforts was convening a transition team of local and national field experts to provide additional depth to my findings.

There were three focal points to the mission of the transition team: Teaching and Learning – responsible for determining the current state of efforts being made to ensure equitable access to high-quality instruction in schools throughout the district; Partnerships – responsible for evaluating the extent to which the district is leveraging key partnerships throughout the community in pursuit of resources that can improve student achievement; and Communications – responsible for identifying the quantity and quality of both internal and external communication channels that exist for the district, including traditional media outlets, social media, knowledge management systems, and community engagement.

Through these transition activities, I collected both quantitative and qualitative data that informed my initial assessment of the district's current state.

ferebee

objective 1

TEACHING AND LEARNING

It was very clear early in my transition that our greatest asset in the IPS community is our people.

We are very fortunate to have committed adults serving students that are excited about learning and focused on preparing for a bright future. Through the service of our educators, support staff and community partners, coupled with the efforts of our students and families, IPS has shown steady improvements in state assessments and the graduation rate. Despite having several schools with a D or an F accountability grade due to not increasing proficiency above the 60% bar, over the past three years increases in ISTEP proficiency have steadily surpassed improvements in state averages. While student growth has been trending upward, the number of schools persistently underachieving and the disproportionate number of students graduating with waivers is concerning. All IPS students should have access to a high-performing school, and students must graduate with the skills needed for career or college.

To realize excellence in all of our schools and for all of our students, professional learning for the adults serving our students must remain at the forefront. It appears that most of the professional development provided for staff has been provided by external contracts, leaving performance cliffs when the providers are gone. To achieve dramatic transformation of student outcomes, internally driven professional learning must be enhanced and expanded. A growth opportunity noted is the need to develop an extensive professional learning plan tightly aligned to a needs assessment toward district achievement goals and academic priorities. The current professional learning plan is not strategic or comprehensive and lacks foci. For example, professional learning opportunities are planned on a monthly basis two months in advance with a sporadic schedule of offerings not well communicated or connected. In addition, the offerings are determined and led by mostly central service teams, incorporating limited teacher voice. Teacher leadership should be a major lever for developing professional learning offerings, content delivery, job-embedded coaching and organized peer learning. Empowering staff and capitalizing on the talents of our most effective educators are critical to accelerate and sustain high-performing schools.

Other strengths observed are opportunities for flexible grouping and differentiated instruction. Most instructional student groups appear to be organized thoughtfully to differentiate learning. For example, I have seen evidence of skills-based small group instruction and data walls to inform corrective instruction. However, there does not appear to be strong alignment between these activities and formative assessment outcomes. Learning activities do not always appear to be aligned with instructional outcomes and represent state standards. Furthermore, I have seen evidence of collaborative planning, but without a focus on

formative assessments. Developing and administering quality formative assessments to inform instruction is a growth opportunity and should be embedded in an instructional planning model district-wide. This approach will improve student performance and engagement.

Student engagement is another area of concern, particularly at the secondary level. Learning activities observed were moderately engaging and challenging. Often times, learning resources and lesson structures were appropriate but lacked variety. There seems to be a rigid focus on test prep and teaching to the test (ISTEP or ECA).* More rigorous learning activities are needed to develop critical thinking and problem solving skills needed for career and college.

A perceived strength for the school district is our magnet and choice options. The unique and specific curriculum offerings for the magnet and choice options are appealing, appreciated and higher achieving; and an underlining strong point is curriculum flexibility and stronger teacher "buy-in" to school curriculum documents as compared to our traditional boundary schools. The scope and sequence of the curriculum documents employed by our traditional schools lack teacher ownership, resulting in a diminishing return on student outcomes. District curriculum documents are perceived to be mostly prescriptive, lack focus on main ideas and provide insufficient references to exemplars. For example, the calibration between curriculum pacing, sequence of state standards and formative assessments is unclear, and the alignment of instructional resources to the pacing guides lacks clarity. It is recommended that new curriculum documents be developed in concert with the adoption of new state standards, ones that are teacher-developed, more agile and connected to professional learning modules.

4 ▶ ferebee

---

*ISTEP stands for Indiana Statewide Testing for Educational Progress.
ECA stands for End of Course Assessment.

objective 2

BOARD-SUPERINTENDENT RELATIONS

IPS is fortunate to have seven dedicated and progressive public servants as Commissioners who represent students, families and the greater community.

The diverse makeup and viewpoints of our Commissioners is an embedded strength. Another major strength for Board of Commissioners and Superintendent relations is the mutual commitment the Board and I share toward cultivating a collaborative, transparent and productive governance team. To deepen and broaden relations with Board members, I have engaged in numerous one-on-one meetings throughout my 100-day transition. To solidify our foundation for productivity, the Board and I examined current protocols and processes for district governance and addressing constituent services.

From our assessments, it was determined that there is strong local policy language addressing the roles of the Board and constituents. For example, there is local policy on reporting patron complaints and positive experiences in addition to provisions for constituents to make comments to the Board on service and other IPS-related concerns or issues. There is local policy addressing transparency and open communications with constituents that should be considered for an update. Another growth opportunity is collecting perception data from our student and families on our services. Currently, there are limited opportunities for constituents to assess and report on district services. Understanding clearly from our stakeholders our strengths and challenges is critical to continuous improvement.

An effective school district includes a collaborative, trusting and productive governance team. To monitor the progress of the relationships among the governance team members, IPS partnered with K12 *Insight* to conduct a Board Governance Survey. The survey is designed to measure Board relationships at the beginning of the school year (pre-assessment), during the school year (mid-year assessment) and at the end of the school year (post-assessment). This report provides the pre-assessment results. The pre-assessment measured Superintendent-to-Board relationships, relationships among Board members and preferred communication from the perspective of School Board members prior to the arrival of the newly appointed Superintendent. Commissioners completed the pre-assessment in November 2013 and the mid-year assessment in January 2014, and will participate in the post-assessment in June 2014. After synthesizing the data from the pre-assessment and Board retreats, the following three growth opportunities were identified: 1) lack of mutual trust and respect among Board members was identified as a challenge for governance relations; 2) there are perceived inconsistencies in the volume, quality and integrity of information Board members receive from the administration; and 3) strategic priorities are needed to guide the work of the governance team. It is important to note that the mid-year assessment marked significantly

5 ▷ ferebee

stronger communication and relations between the Board of Commissioners and me.

In addition to the aforementioned three areas for improvement, the governance team identified our meeting time as a productivity barrier. As a result, we recently revised our Board meeting structure and agenda development processes. For example, action and briefing sessions have been streamlined, and a quarterly retreat schedule was established. This redesign has yielded more focused and strategic outcomes and meeting time. It is also recommended that the governance team move to a legislative working group model to transition from a buy-in model to an ownership model to determine the IPS legislative agenda. This ad hoc approach will accelerate efforts required for complex critical initiatives through targeted collaboration and empower leaders while building capacity throughout the organization via distributive leadership.

ferebee

objective 3

REORGANIZATION FOR EFFECTIVENESS

While progress has been made and some organizational moves have impacted school-based staff, IPS hasn't dramatically shifted the organization of central services over the past decade.

The organization of central services reflects the same structures of a much larger student population for IPS compared to the decreased enrollment numbers of today. Over the past decade, IPS enrollment numbers have decreased by approximately 10,000 students. Teaching and school-based support staff have been significantly reduced due to declining enrollment; however, central service staffing has remained consistent. In addition to this imbalance, central services departments have been perceived as inefficient and convoluted. For example, clear lines of reporting and supervision were not evident, and there was a lack of ownership for district outcomes and shortcomings, resulting in talent gaps. For instance, instead of moving ineffective school-based staff out of school leadership roles, many were moved to district leadership, weakening performance management structures and opportunities for progress.

During my entry period, I reviewed organizational charts and studied core leadership workflow to assess productivity. After my analysis in concert with the Board of Commissioners, core leadership was reorganized to enhance opportunities to right-size central service teams, heighten district-wide efficiency and effectiveness and decrease the need for middle management. Deputy positions for academics and operations were established while reducing the number of direct reports to the Superintendent to streamline communication and decision-making. A chief strategist position has been established to serve as the lead architect for transformation. Academic improvement officer roles were created to widen the scope of responsibilities for supervision of schools and principals and reduce redundancy of district academic leadership. Other executive roles were eliminated or repurposed to better align talent with our greatest needs and increase agility. Reorganization is in process for the majority of the central services divisions and will be complete during the 2014-2015 school year. It is important to note that initial phases of academic and facilities management divisions were complete during my entry plan period. This flattened leadership design achieved three critical needs: 1) reduced bureaucratic layers for schools and families; 2) advanced organizational capacity; and 3) elevated ownership and accountability.

*my*IPS

objective 4

COLLABORATIVE COMMUNICATIONS

The former IPS Office of School and Community Relations is now the Public Relations Division and will employ highly skilled individuals talented in media relations, editorial content, public relations and digital marketing to support strategic communications efforts.

Strong communication and stakeholder engagement is the cornerstone of realizing maximum community support. We must maintain two-way communication with our entire community, including those members who are not directly impacted by IPS services. An inability to communicate effectively with internal and external stakeholders often poses challenges for educating our students at the highest levels. While there is overwhelming community interest in supporting IPS, the bridge of communication is a perceived impediment for our stakeholders and families. Currently, there is no district road map for providing clear and intentional messages to our varied audiences. For example, a strategic communication plan template does not exist, yet it is greatly needed to further outreach efforts. Procedures and protocols are needed to manage and support outreach efforts at the school level. School-based employees play a critical role in branding, marketing and messaging to school and district audiences. A thorough district-wide communication plan will be developed to lower barriers between IPS, our families and the community at large. This comprehensive plan will address specific outreach goals with detailed means of monitoring communication and public relations efforts.

Another challenge identified is the need to dramatically improve the image of IPS and our offerings. It seems many stakeholders and reporters have misconceptions that most IPS students are troubled and/or IPS schools are all unruly and lack quality. One way to improve media coverage of IPS is to meet with local newspaper editorial boards and television stations to discuss how IPS is being covered. The administration has initiated these talks by hosting a meeting with leaders of local media outlets, editorial boards and education reports to establish a framework for collaboration. In addition, the administration will facilitate monthly media briefings on key topics to deliver vital strategic information to stakeholders via a variety of communication modes. An overarching media relations plan will provide an opportunity to bolster and monitor coverage and improve viewpoint credibility.

While much outward-facing work can be done to combat negative IPS stereotypes and enhance stakeholder engagement, even more laser-like focus must be placed on internal efforts. Strong communication starts within, and tremendous power can be found in robust internal marketing and branding efforts. Professional development opportunities will be provided to improve core and school leadership capacity for improving messaging and marketing. Strengthened communication for IPS will foster brand awareness, improved customer service and positive student outcomes. In this regard, social media outreach is a growing strength

ferebee

for IPS. Social media outreach efforts are well-managed, and a staff person is dedicated to this area. Social media and Internet platforms are major channels for widening access and awareness. To this end, IPS will also restyle the district and school Web site to enrich functionality, look and feel.

ferebee

*my*IPS

objective 5

STRATEGIC PLANNING

The current IPS strategic plan is evidence of a creditable effort to establish district goals to advance the district mission of preparing and empowering all students for life.

While the 2010-2015 plan provides academic and operational aims and offers benchmarks for success, its metrics are in some ways misaligned to its broad targets. In my listening, observation and learning, I have seen that there is a need to adjust and clarify our goals in order to have a better plan for realizing our powerful and relevant vision: "IPS will be the flagship in innovative urban education, preparing all students to be successful in the global economy." While synthesizing the many data points from my exploratory efforts has been underway (i.e., community work sessions and town hall meetings, student talks, staff meetings, stakeholder survey, Twitter chats, one-on-one meetings, business and community group meetings, etc.), a district strategic plan design process has been developed. The development of the next IPS strategic plan will include a collaboration between governance, administrative and community representatives and incorporate various quantitative and qualitative data to ensure significantly improved organizational effectiveness in the coming years.

Sound financial strategy is vital to the productivity of any organization, and this is another growth opportunity for IPS. Thorough financial planning is critical, as budget limitations have been a prominent perceived barrier to district success and student outcomes. During my entry period, I reviewed the school corporation's financial projections, resource allocations and practices for building the annual operating budget. My review provided two key findings. First, there was no documentation of any type of reconciliation reporting comparing projected and actual revenues and expenditures. The lack of reconciliation reporting is evidence of diminished budget transparency and has resulted in misperception of the district's actual financial status. Secondly, most departmental budgets were consistent from year to year and were not aligned to strategic priorities. This misalignment challenges efficient spending and limits progress and innovation. Going forward, monthly reconciliation of our projected versus actual expenditures and revenues will be reported quarterly, and expenditures will be aligned to strategic planning efforts in a reengineered, transparent and inclusive budget development process. For example, a budget development committee representing various stakeholders will be convened to engage the community in the financial planning process to enhance strategy, ownership and transparency.

The next IPS strategic plan will ensure that academic and operational aims are clear and representative of the most critical district priorities. Additionally, financial allocations will be tightly aligned to strategic plan goals and objectives. Metrics will be designed, and progress will be consistently monitored so that

10   ferebee

acceleration and corrective action can be easily employed through continuous improvement processes. Organizational development efforts will be implemented to ensure that each employee can clearly articulate our vision and mission and fully understands his/her role in moving IPS forward. Individuals' professional development will be aligned to the advancement of the organization. Strategies will be employed to help employees become IPS ambassadors – they will be empowered to participate in school and departmental planning, contribute to monitoring, reporting and celebratory efforts and discuss the state of the district with whomever they come in contact.

*my***IPS**

summary table

Great efforts are quickly diminished when no one asks the question, "Now what?" Below listed by objective is a summary of next steps to mobilize action resulting from my findings.

OBJECTIVE	NEXT STEP 1	NEXT STEP 2	NEXT STEP 3	PROJECTED TIMELINE
1	Reengineer professional learning model	Establish specific and measurable performance targets	Reformat curriculum documents and formative assessment tools	August 2014
2	Administer end-of-year governance survey	Explore leadership development opportunities aligned with organizational growth		June 2014
3	Finalize central services organizational structure	Facilitate summer leadership institute for school and district leadership		August 2014
4	Launch district and school Web site redesign			August 2014
5	Provide strategic thinking training modules for governance team	Conduct a strategic planning retreat with core leadership to deepen understanding of planning processes		September 2014

 myIPS

significant milestones

My initial days in the district have been very rewarding. I have spent a great deal of time synthesizing a wealth of information from varied sources about the IPS community. In order to gain well-rounded perspective, I scheduled my active and reflective time strategically. Some of my planned deliverables were completed ahead of schedule, and some were delayed. Below is a chart illustrating the number of significant milestones completed during my first 100 days.

SCHEDULE

	11/1	11/22	12/3	12/17	1/30	2/28
ENTRY PLAN OBJECTIVE	30	45	50	60	80	100
OBJECTIVE 1	4			3		3
OBJECTIVE 2	3				4	3
OBJECTIVE 3	4		1	1		2
OBJECTIVE 4		2			2	2
OBJECTIVE 5	2			2		2
TOTAL	13	2	1	6	6	12
GRAND TOTAL						40

stakeholders

Working collaboratively with stakeholders is the only way to facilitate comprehensive transformation. Ownership of challenges and solutions begins with transparent two-way communications. While I have spent a great deal of time reviewing data, I have most enjoyed my conversations with those who support and are supported by IPS. The schematic below reflects my stakeholder touch points.

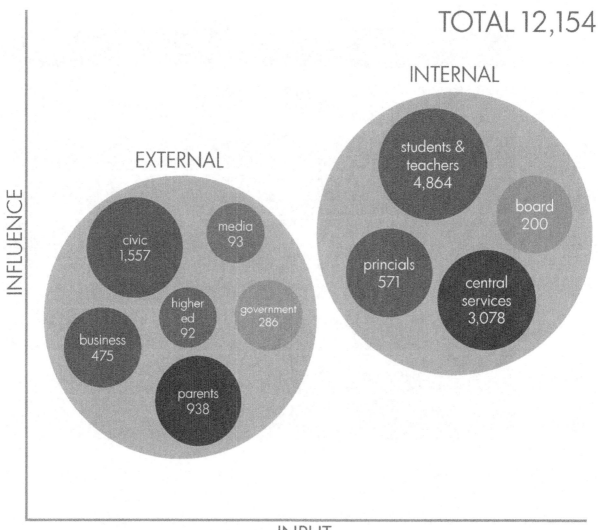

TOTAL 12,154

INTERNAL

students & teachers
4,864

board
200

princials
571

central services
3,078

EXTERNAL

civic
1,557

media
93

higher ed
92

government
286

business
475

parents
938

INFLUENCE

INPUT

14 ferebee

myIPS

artifact 1

During the course of my entry plan, I developed a pacing guide to track my progress toward completion of the actions aligned with my objectives. Below is a snapshot of my tracking matrix illustrating scheduled deliverables for Objectives 1 and 2.

tracking
superintendent's entry plan

	legend	
objective	*	stated in published entry plan
1 vcd	c	complete
2 Improve Board-Superintendent relations by cultivating a collaborative, trusting and productive governance team.	ip	in progress
3 Reorganize the district's support model to enhance efficiency and effectiveness.	ed	extended duration
4 Establish effective communication structures to build supportive and collaborative stakeholder relationships.	ns	not started
5 Develop a framework for a comprehensive strategic planning process building on the district's 2010-2015 Plan.	q-note	quick note
0 Other	t/g/ct	transition/governance/core leadership team

ticker tape: *days = actions = percent • 0 = 0 - 0% • 30 = 10 = 25% • 60 = 20 = 50% • 90 = 30 = 75% • 100 = 40 = 100%*

action			11/1 30	11/7 45	12/9 50	12/1 60	1/30 80	2/28 100	product	delegate	evaluator	status	q-note
1	1.1	Assess professional learning plans & needs for alignment							bullet points	legrand (.5)	ferebee	c	comprehensive plan needed
2	1.2	Conduct learning walks to observe instructional & professional learning communities - 30 (ongoing)							summary		ferebee	c	observations through weekly site visits
3	1.3	*Analyze patterns in student achievement to identify trends in performance							bullet points	roach (.5)	ferebee	c	2012-13 data not formally approved
4	1.4	*Review curriculum documents (curriculum maps, pacing guides & monitoring rubrics) to assess curriculum alignment							bullet points	legrand (.5)	ferebee	c	magnet and inetwork schools are exempt from following district guides
5	1.5	*Administer survey to assess strengths & opportunities for improvement							results/report		t team	ip	identified survey tool (K12 insight)
6	1.6	*Evaluate formative assessment processes to ensure mastery of student learning							bullet points		t team	c	acuity results align with ISTEP results
7	1.7	Conduct learning walks to observe instructional & professional learning communities - 60 (ongoing)							summary		t team	c	observations through weekly site visits
8	1.8	*Meet with instructional leadership team to conduct SWOT analysis							SWOT document		t team	ns	
9	1.9	*Host focus groups of stakeholders to assess instructional program							summary		t team	ip	
10	1.10	Conduct learning walks to observe instructional & professional learning communities - 100 (ongoing)							summary		t team	ip	observations through weekly site visits
11	2.1	*Examine the current protocols & processes for addressing constituent services							bullet points	pfeiffer (.25)	g team	c	policy review in process
12	2.2	*Administer Board-Superintendent perception pre-assessment to evaluate Board-Superintendent relations							results report	boler (.25)	g team	c	draft survey questions developed. will administer survey after initial retreat
13	2.3	Engage in one-on-one meetings with Board members to deepen relationships & broaden							bullet points		g team	c	met with 6 of 7 Board members
14	2.4	*Meet with Board president & vice president to establish a regular meeting schedule to develop Board meeting & retreat agendas & to discussing district matters							calendar, templates, processes		g team	c	regular meeting schedule with president established
15	2.5	Review Board election process to ensure continuity of governance team							bullet points		g team	c	elections in January
16	2.6	*Hold first Board retreat to discuss communication protocols, roles & responsibilities, norms & expectations for first year & agenda setting							protocols, summary		g team	c	retreat scheduled for 10/30/13
17	2.7	Engage in one-on-one meetings with Board members to deepen relationships & broaden							bullet points		g team	ip	
18	2.8	*Host second retreat to establish a performance evaluation format & district goals							summary		g team	ns	
19	2.9	*Administer Board-Superintendent perception post-assessment to evaluate Board-Superintendent relations							results report		g team	ns	
20	2.10	Engage in one-on-one meetings with Board members to deepen relationships & broaden perspectives (ongoing)							bullet points		g team	ip	
21	3.1	*Identify and hire critical new team members to join core leadership									ferebee	c	legrand & boler; see artifacts; academics reorg in

IPS   R/lb; r. 5/2/2014/ 3:42 PM

15 ▶ ferebee

myIPS

artifact 2

Considering qualitative information is just as critical as – sometimes more so than – examining facts and figures. During my time spent in classrooms and planning sessions, I captured empirical data by using my "Ferebee's Five or Scribe" tool. I completed this electronic form on a mobile device to quickly record up to five succinct points or two short paragraphs from an observation or a review. Below is a snapshot of an entry I generated that correlates to Objective 1 Action 7 (see tracking document).

product
superintendent's entry plan

5

list		i.d.# 1.7
•		
•		
•		
•		
•		

scribe
i.d. # 1.7

Schools implementing the 8-step process with fidelity seem to have more purposeful professional learning communities. Learning targets seem to be unclear for many students, which poses a challenge for mastery and ownership. In a few classrooms, learning targets are either posted or discussed. When asked, students struggle with explaining their learning targets in detail. Collaborative planning for teachers is a growth opportunity for the district. I see limited consistency among teachers teaching the same course or grade level. There are limited opportunities for teachers to share best practices across grade levels and content areas. This need should be addressed in our comprehensive professional learning plan and can be accomplished after school and summer. There is a willingness among teachers to plan together early before school starts. Most teachers observed appear to be managing their instructional time well, high time on-task noted.

IPS   ferebee's five or scribe   1.7

artifact 3

Data drives our continuous improvement processes; therefore, it is important to be able to aggregate and disaggregate information as needed. Below is a snapshot of a concise data summary of assessment progress.

Summary of Progress Towards IPS Strategic Goals

ISTEP+ Goals

The goals set for Grades 7 and 8 indicate different targets by subject area with a 5 point increase in performance expected each successive year.   While IPS has continued to show improvement each year, unfortunately it has not been to the level or at the rate expected to meet the goals set as indicted in the chart below.

ISTEP+ Gr 7-8	ELA Target	ELA Attained	ELA Diff	Math Target	Math Attained	Math Diff
2010-11	50	47.4	(2.6)	60	48.8	(11.2)
2011-12	55	48	(7.0)	65	57.4	(7.6)
2012-13	60	51.2	(8.8)	70	59.8	(10.2)

The goals set for Grades 3-6 could have been interpreted as being the same for both English and Math or as being the expected performance for how many students should pass both subjects. The chart below shows both interpretations. Unfortunately, again, while IPS continues to show increases in performance, it is not at the level or rate necessary to meet the expected goals.

ISTEP+ Gr 3-8	Ela Target	Ela Attained	Ela Diff	Math Target	Math Attained	Math Diff	Both Target	Both Attained	Both Diff
2010-11	65	59.7	(5.3)	65	61.4	(3.6)	65	47.9	(17.1)
2011-12	70	62.9	(7.1)	70	64.8	(5.2)	70	51.3	(18.7)
2012-13	75	62.1	(12.9)	75	67.9	(7.1)	75	53.6	(21.4)

The goals set for Science are different for each grade with 5 point increases expected at Grade 4 and a steeper 10 point increase for the first year and an 8 point increase for the second at Grade 6. Unfortunately our performance in science has not shown steady increases and our progressions towards the targets have fallen further behind as indicated below.

ISTEP+ Science Gr 4 and 6	Gr 4 Science Target	Gr 4 Science Attained	Gr 4 Science Diff	Gr 6 Science Target	Gr 6 Science Attained	Gr 6 Science Diff
2010-11	65	50.7	(14.3)	42	32	(10.0)
2011-12	70	54.7	(15.3)	52	32	(20.0)
2012-13	75	47.4	(27.6)	60	38.4	(21.6)

artifact 4

As previously stated, strong collaboration between the Board and the Superintendent is required to achieve marked success in the district. Some of the work of our governance team included reviewing, revising and establishing processes. Below are snapshots illustrating the collaboration of governance team members to restructure meetings for increased efficiency and community engagement.

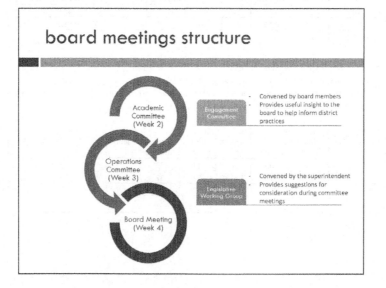

artifact 5

Students are our most valuable resource. Their voices are guiding, affirming and inspiring. While conducting classroom meetings with students across the district, it was important for me to remind students to always keep the conversation going around what works well, what needs improvement and what innovative ideas can be implemented in IPS. Below is a front-and-back snapshot of a bookmark that I continue to hand to students to encourage reading (and sharing). The back of the bookmark highlights district social media handles as well as a hashtag used for district-hosted Twitter events and general postings about followers' IPS experiences. The bookmark was also distributed in Spanish.

   ferebee

ENTRY PLAN

Lewis D. Ferebee, Ed.D.
Indianapolis Public Schools

September 27, 2013

introduction and purpose

Thoughtful and purposeful transition activities are vital to the organizational development of a school district. With great consideration, I have designed this entry plan to guide my work as I employ a proactive, focused, and strategic approach to leading Indianapolis Public Schools (IPS).

The purpose of this entry plan is to present my initial goals and the actions and anticipated outcomes associated with what I feel will result in a successful transition into the role of Superintendent. This plan is anchored by my leadership philosophy of listening broadly and deeply to the voices of stakeholders and learning more about the school district's strengths and impediments. This practice will allow me to begin assessing the organization's agility and opportunities for improvement while engaging the community in shaping our compelling and relevant vision for the future of IPS. I believe dramatic district transformation requires that we engage everyone; it is important that we build community ownership, rather than later request buy-in.

The transition activities outlined in this entry plan are designed to enable me to achieve the following five goals:

1) gather information carefully about the organization and community;

2) establish a strong community presence early;

3) assess the state of the school district while gaining historical perspective;

4) identify critical challenges and opportunities; and

5) build on strengths by creating a supportive network of critical friends to the district and leveraging resources that will help advance Indianapolis Public Schools.

Specific objectives associated with these goals and a projected timeline of activities for my first 100 days as Superintendent are included herein.

objective 1

Assess the strengths and opportunities for improvement in the district's instructional program.

30 Days:
Observations: curriculum documents, achievement data, and school visits

60 Days:
Summary of instructional focus group (embedded in online survey as well)

100 Days:
Strengths, Weaknesses, Opportunities and Threats (SWOT) analysis of IPS instructional program

actions will include:

Analyze patterns in student achievement to identify trends in performance

Administer survey to assess strengths and opportunities for improvement

Meet with instructional leadership team to conduct SWOT analysis

Review curriculum documents (curriculum maps, pacing guides and monitoring rubrics) to assess curriculum alignment

Evaluate formative assessment processes to ensure mastery of student learning

Host focus groups of stakeholders to assess instructional program

3 ferebee

objective 2

Improve Board-Superintendent relations by cultivating a collaborative, trusting and productive governance team.

30 Days:
Summary of pre-assessment results and communication protocols

80 Days:
Governance guiding principles

100 Days:
Perception survey data: Governance team relations; Performance evaluation format consistent with Board policy and statutory requirements

actions will include:

Examine the current protocols and processes for addressing constituent services

Meet with Board president and vice president to establish a regular meeting schedule to develop Board meeting and retreat agendas and to discuss district matters

Host second retreat to establish a performance evaluation format and district goals

Administer Board-Superintendent perception pre-assessment to evaluate Board-Superintendent relations

Hold first Board retreat to discuss communication protocols, roles and responsibilities, norms and expectations for first year and agenda setting

Administer Board-Superintendent perception post-assessment to evaluate Board-Superintendent relations

 ferebee

 my**IPS**

objective 3

Reorganize the district's support model to enhance efficiency and effectiveness.

30 Days:
Complete phase I of re-organization and staff study; Report on current funding for central services positions

60 Days:
Assessment of current structure (embedded in online survey); Potential personnel savings attached with proposed structure

100 Days:
Revised organizational support model; Cost savings for new structure

actions will include:

Identify and hire critical new team members to join core leadership

Administer survey to assess efficiency and effectiveness of central services

Review all organizational charts and other related documents

Request briefing papers from all division leaders providing an overview of their current areas of responsibility, major initiatives underway with projected timelines, a review of significant or potential problems in each area of responsibility and major decisions needing to be made in one month, three months and six months

Review district's financial projections, resource allocations and the process for building the annual operating budget

Review draft of revised organizational model with Board for feedback and suggestions

5 ferebee

objective 4

Establish effective communication structures to build supportive and collaborative stakeholder relationships.

45 Days:
Communication SWOT analysis

80 Days:
Communication protocols for leadership (embedded in online survey)

100 Days:
Standard Operating Procedures for communication; Process for establishing student, teacher, principal and business advisory councils

actions will include:

Review processes and systems that guide district communication to better understand outreach efforts

Administer survey to assess effectiveness of current communication strategies

Provide training to core leadership on developing operating procedures to enhance staff capacity

Conduct a review of the services provided by the Office of School and Community Relations to assess the quality and effectiveness of district communications

Meet with leaders of local media outlets, editorial boards and education reporters to establish a framework for collaboration

Conduct a communication protocols planning retreat to support the development of operating procedures

6 ▷ ferebee

objective 5

Develop a comprehensive strategic planning framework building on the district's 2010-2015 Plan.

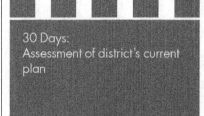

30 Days:
Assessment of district's current plan

60 Days:
Presentation to the Board on draft process

100 Days:
Strategic plan development process

actions will include:

Review processes and systems that align the distribution of resources with strategic priorities to identify potential process improvement

Conduct a strategic plan retreat with core leadership to deepen understanding of planning processes

Align strategic planning process with advanced principles of organizational development and continuous improvement to ensure strong plan development

Evaluate performance towards meeting strategic plan goals to assess effectiveness of current strategies

Provide professional learning opportunities for Board members on strategic planning to deepen understanding of planning processes

Establish a communications plan to engage and empower stakeholders in the plan development process and implementation

7 ferebee

milestones

The previous five pages outline the specific objectives I aim to accomplish as I enter Indianapolis Public Schools. The information has been synthesized by date and is provided below in a supplemental calendar format which highlights entry plan milestones from Day One, September 23, 2013 to Day One-Hundred, February 28, 2014. This calendar takes into account district holidays and winter break.

DAY 1	DAY 10	DAY 15	DAY 20
SEPTEMBER 23	OCTOBER 4	OCTOBER 11	OCTOBER 18
First day as Indianapolis Public Schools' Superintendent			
DAY 25	**DAY 30**	**DAY 35**	**DAY 40**
OCTOBER 25	NOVEMBER 1	NOVEMBER 8	NOVEMBER 15
	30 day milestones achieved for Goals 1, 2, 3 and 5		
DAY 45	**DAY 50**	**DAY 55**	**DAY 60**
NOVEMBER 22	DECEMBER 3	DECEMBER 10	DECEMBER 17
45 day milestone achieved for Goal 4	Internal briefing		60 day milestones achieved for Goals 1, 3 and 5
DAY 65	**DAY 70**	**DAY 75**	**DAY 80**
JANUARY 8	JANUARY 15	JANUARY 23	JANUARY 30
			80 day milestones achieved for Goals 2 and 4
DAY 85	**DAY 90**	**DAY 95**	**DAY 100**
FEBRUARY 6	FEBRUARY 13	FEBRUARY 21	FEBRUARY 28
			100 day milestones achieved for Goals 1, 2, 3, 4 and 5

timeline

Over my first one-hundred days, it is imperative to make significant progress toward accomplishing my entry goals. Though I will guide the activities that will aid in completing the five objectives, success will certainly be the result of a team effort. The Indianapolis Chamber of Commerce partners with IPS to conduct an extensive departmental assessment to gain insight into district operational practices. Work on this initiative is already underway and will help to inform our planning efforts. Additionally, I will convene a team of national and local subject matter experts to review specific internal and external components that are highly impactful to district success. Members of this Transition Team will visit the district in the coming months to evaluate teaching and learning, culture and context, strategic partnerships and communications, among other things. The team will cite their research and provide helpful recommendations for improvement.

Within 30 days of entering the district, I aim to complete approximately 10 key actions (or 25% of the work that is specified in the entry plan). By my 60th day, I expect to complete half of the actions in the entry plan. Within 90 days, I should complete approximately 30 of 40 key actions (or 75%).

This information is aligned with the preceding calendar of milestones; however, it depicts completion status on a continuum for at-a-glance progress monitoring.

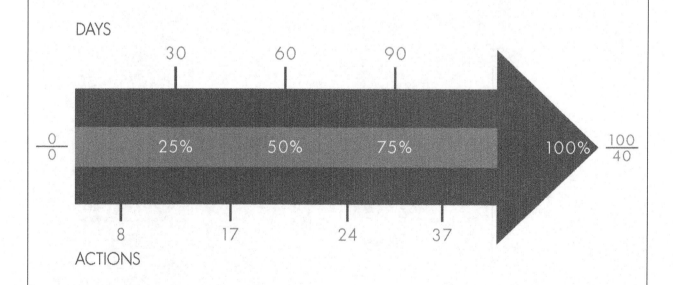

effort

I believe that building capacity is essential to nurturing student learning and refining adult collegial relationships. Below, I provide insight into how I process what is required of me to successfully accomplish my entry plan goals. This diagram depicts how I will allocate my energy toward five integral components that are essential to an effective transition: Gathering stakeholder feedback; Conducting an environmental scan; Creating culture; Developing a strategic plan framework; and Reorganizing for effectiveness and efficiency. As illustrated, I will place a great deal of effort on listening and learning.

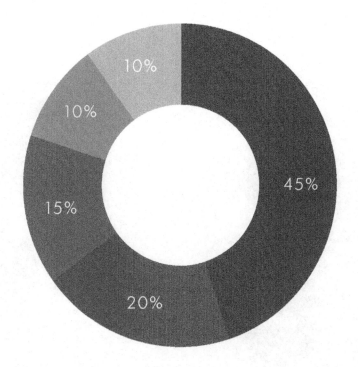

 GATHER STAKEHOLDER FEEDBACK

 CONDUCT ENVIROMENTAL SCAN

 CREATE CULTURE

 DEVELOP STRATEGIC PLAN FRAMEWORK

REORGANIZE FOR EFFECTIVENESS & EFFICIENCY

 ferebee

stakeholders

While conducting an environmental scan, it is critical to understand the current climate and its itinerant circles of influence. This is necessary in order to enhance organizational effectiveness and ultimately gain competitive intelligence. The strategic diagram below illustrates the potential relationship between internal and external stakeholder groups in terms of their broad participation levels and influence on district operations. This diagram is not intended to be an accurate assessment of current stakeholder engagement, rather it highlights the importance of including stakeholder groups in our planning endeavors.

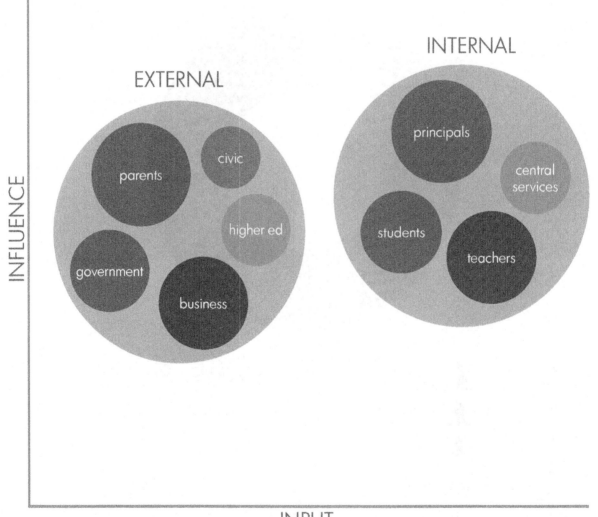

ferebee

www.myips.org

June 24, 2014

ferebee

Questions

1. How many of the goals in the Entry Plan are aimed at addressing internal issues? Which goals are those?
2. How many of the goals in the Entry Plan address external issues? Which goals are those?
3. In his interviews, Dr. Ferebee stated that IPS needs to provide alternative programs that meet the needs of the students and families the district serves. In what way(s), does the process outlined in the Entry Plan indicate that IPS is taking steps to identify and meet the needs of its customers?
4. What additional goal(s) would you add to the 100-Day Entry Plan to help IPS better meet the needs of its customers? What additional objective(s) would you add to the Entry Plan to help meet the additional goal(s) and how would you achieve those objectives in a 30-, 60-, and 100-day time frame?

Applying the Concepts

1. Prepare a perceptual map of your own school and its competitor schools and analyze it. Are any of your competitors attempting to occupy the same (or similar) positions as your school? Can you identify any gaps? If so, suggest a program or other plan of action on how your school can fill that gap.
2. Write a positioning statement either for your school or a specific program offered by your school (or district) that accurately reflects the target audience you are seeking to serve, their need, and the point of differentiation.
3. Talk to people not involved with your school or district, ask them how they would describe your school (or the schools in your district) to someone who was new to town and looking to enroll their children in a local school. Does their perception match your perception? Do the same exercise for some of your competitor schools.

References

American Red Cross. (2013). Benefits of Donating. Retrieved from http://www.redcrossblood.org/donating-blood

Armstrong, G., & Kotler, P. (2013). *Marketing: An Introduction* (11th ed.). Boston, MA: Pearson.

Calder, B., & Reagan, S. (2001). "Brand Design," in D. Iacobucci, (Ed.), *Kellogg on Marketing.* New York: John Wiley & Sons.

Cross, C. T. (2010). *Political Education: National Policy Comes of Age.* NY: Teachers College Press.

Daye, D. (2012). Brand positioning statement example: Zipcar. Retrieved from http://www.brandingstrategyinsider.com/2012/04/brand-positioning-statement-example-zipcar.html

Henderson, A. T., Mapp, K. L., Johnson, V. R., & Davies, D. (2007). *Beyond the Bake Sale.* New York: The New Press.

Hilton Worldwide. (2013). Summary of Brands. Retrieved from http://hiltonworldwide.com/portfolio/

Kotler, P. (1988). *Marketing Management: Analysis, Planning, Implementation and Control* (6th ed.). Englewood Cliffs, NJ: Prentice Hall.

Murrell, P. C. (2001). *The community teacher: A framework for effective urban teaching.* New York: Teacher's College Press.

Porter, M. (1980). *Competitive Strategy: Techniques for Analyzing Industries and Competitors.* New York: Free Press.

Procter & Gamble. (2013). Retrieved from http://www.pg.com/en_US/company/purpose_people/index.shtml

Ries, A., & Trout, J. (1982). *Positioning: The Battle for Your Mind.* New York: Warner Books.

Robinson, C. K. (2012). Peter Drucker on marketing: Application and implications for libraries. *Managing Library Finance, 25,* 4–12.

Schulyer, M. A. (2001). *Mail @ the Millennium: Will the postal service go private?* Washington, DC: The Cato Institute.

Smiley, A. D., Howland, A. A., & Anderson, J. A. (2008). Cultural brokering as a core practice of a special education parent liaison program in a large urban school district. *Journal of Urban Learning, Teaching and Research, 4,* 86–95.

Smith, W. R. (1956). Product differentiation and market segmentation as alternative marketing strategies. *Journal of Marketing, 21*(1), 3–8.

Solomon, M. (2004). *Consumer Behavior: Buying. Having and Being (6th ed.).* Upper Saddle River, NJ: Pearson, Prentice Hall.

http://www.wthr.com/story/23812546/2013/10/28/new-ips-superintendent-listening-learning-in-schools

http://praiseindy.com/1920824/exclusive-in-his-1st-live-radio-interview-new-ips-supt-dr-lewis-ferebee-talks-his-goals-for-his-100-days-wants-to-listenlearn/

http://www.ips.k12.in.us/wp-content/uploads/2013/09/Dr.-Lewis-D.-Ferebees-Entry-Plan.pdf

Chapter 2

Educational Consumers

Don't find customers for your products, find products for your customers.

–Seth Godin, American Author and Entrepreneur

Who Are Educational Consumers?

Previously, back to school shopping meant buying school supplies and uniforms, but in today's world, school shoppers are taking a more consumer-like approach to the school selection process. School

Creativa Images/Shutterstock.com

shoppers are becoming more savvy and growing in numbers. In 2004, the Washington DC Opportunity Scholarship program gave choice scholarships to over 1,700 public school students whose families were navigating poverty, as a way for them to pursue a nonpublic education for their children (Wolf et al., 2010). The program has grown considerably and now serves more than 8,400 students. A study by Michigan Future Inc., (2012) found that more than 71% of Detroit Public School families were shopping for or utilizing school alternatives for their children. Additionally, the Indiana Department of Education released a report documenting more than 9,300 students who obtained a voucher to attend a nonpublic school during the 2012–2013 school year (Damron, 2012). The city of Milwaukee started its school choice programs in 1990. More than 23,000 students now take part in Milwaukee's Parental Choice Program (Wolf, 2012). Currently, there are 18 voucher programs in 12 states, 14 tax-credit scholarship programs in 11 states, an educational savings account system in one state, and six individual tax credit/deduction programs in six states (Friedman Foundation, 2013). In addition to voucher and choice programs, 42 states now have various forms of charter schools. According to the National Alliance for Public Charter Schools (NAPCS) there are more than 5,000 public charter schools across the country serving more than two million students (NAPCS, 2013). According to the National Home Education Research Institute (2013) there are more than two million students being homeschooled and the Council for American Private Education (2013) cites more than five million students attending 33,000 private schools nationally.

These numbers mark a new trend taking place in the field of education. Traditional public schools no longer have a guaranteed market share of students, or tax dollars, based on geographic location and families with little to no options in the past, now have many. Millions of families are no longer sending their students to the school assigned to them based on geographic location. They are looking into options and doing their homework.

In situations where families make purchasing or consumption decisions, a number of variables come into play. Often, parents are charged with the final decision-making authority; however, there are a number of roles family members and others play which can influence the ultimate purchase. Families make two general types of purchase decisions: consensual and accommodative (Davis, 1972). In consensual decisions, all members of the family agree on the selected purchase. Conversely, accommodative decision situations occur when members of the family cannot agree on the purchase, resulting in bargaining, compromise, or coercion. Four types of conflict have been identified (Seymour & Lessne, 1984). The first source of conflict is Interpersonal Need, or the degree of personal involvement associated with the purchase decision. For example, a college student living away from home may not care as much about a household purchase as a child still living at home. The second type of decision conflict is Product Involvement. In other words, a family member who does not use the product, such as a coffee maker or lawn mower, may not care as much about the ultimate decision. The third level of conflict entails Responsibility. For example, the children in the family may be excited about getting a new pet, while the mother may be concerned about having to assume responsibility for the day-to-day care of the animal. Finally, Power has been identified as a source of conflict. This refers to the level of influence exerted by a family member over the others involved in the purchase.

With respect to power or influence, a number of researchers have investigated purchase decisions involving children. Such research has concluded children tend to have more influence in decisions that directly affect them or for products purchased for their own use (Foxman, Tansuhaj, & Ekstrom, 1989). Research involving middle-class families shows children not only play a key role in the purchasing process but parents welcome the input and information children provide (Thomson, Laing, & McKee, 2007). This same research demonstrates the behavior exhibited by children in a family purchase setting. Rather than acting alone, children are more likely to identify a common need for the decision with at least one other member of the family—either other children or a parent. Such coalitions are viewed as more credible and yield greater influence on the ultimate purchasing decision.

Family system theorists study families as a group of people intertwined to create one entity (Nichols & Schwartz, 1994); the theory is used to investigate the impact of individual experiences of a single family member on the dynamics of the entire family unit. In most cases, educational consumers are made of two distinct groups of people, families and students. It is important not to confuse these two as entities as the same target group, but to recognize they influence each other in the educational decision-making process. According to research, families and students appear to be looking for different attributes from schools. Doyle and Feldman (2006) found students chose a school based on academics, support, and school culture. The study also noted students chose to stay in the schools because they provided college and career preparation, teachers who paid attention to academic and emotional needs, and positive student relationships (Doyle & Feldman, 2006). Conversely, it has been found that families were more concerned with class size, quality of instruction, school climate, and a disciplined environment (Bukhari & Randall, 2009). With two types of consumers looking for various attributes, public schools need to develop marketing strategies that aid both groups in their educational decision-making.

Across the country families and students from various walks of life are being provided with educational choices. Many families and students who never had access to educational choices before are now presented with a plethora of options. So who are these families utilizing their educational choice options? According to the National Center of Education Statistics (2010) from 1993 to 2007 several groups trended away from attending their assigned public school. These include: white students, black students, nonpoor students, students whose parents' highest level of education was some college, graduate, or professional education, and two-parent households. These trends were significant across all four regions (North, South, East, West) of the US. The study also found several groups that trended for attending their assigned public schools. These include: Hispanic students, near poor and poor students, students whose parents' highest level of education was high school, GED, or less than a high school education, and one-parent households (NCES, 2010).

Understanding the Decision-Making Process

There are a number of variables affecting consumers' purchasing decisions. These include personal characteristics such as age, occupation, economic situation, and lifestyle. Psychological characteristics also play into purchasing behavior, like personality, motivation, and attitude. Beyond variables more directly tied to the individual, however, there are external factors that can also impact consumer behavior. External factors related to culture include ethnic culture, any sub-cultures to which an individual may belong, as well as social class standing. Finally, social variables including reference groups, family and even the role a person plays in society can affect the types of product purchases. In this section, we will discuss the variables affecting the consumer decision-making, as well as the steps in the purchasing process.

Personal characteristics such as a person's age or stage in life can have an enormous impact on purchasing patterns. Few people in their early 20s are in the market for dentures or support stockings, just as few octogenarians visit nightclubs or download the latest hip-hop song from iTunes. As people move through their lives, needs change, as do the purchases they make to fulfill those needs. It is easy to recognize that not all adults will be making a school "purchasing" decision; only those with school-age children have such a need. Other characteristics of a personal nature include occupation. White collar workers will be more likely to purchase shirts and ties for work, as opposed to blue collar workers who may be more likely to buy heavy work boots or rugged-wear pants. Lifestyle preferences also factor into the types of purchases people make. People who like spending time in the outdoors will be more likely to purchase fishing or camping equipment, for example, than those individuals who enjoy exploring history. This group might be more apt to purchase Civil War books or plan a trip to Gettysburg. Educators need to keep this in mind thinking that sending a comment to the local newspaper, or a speaker to the local Rotary Club might seem like marketing, but it doesn't necessarily hit the right demographic, nor do these "one shot" efforts necessarily work.

Income is another personal characteristic affecting an individual's purchasing decision-making. Those with higher incomes have increased spending capability. However, what that individual does with the increased income can vary widely. Where schools are concerned, for example, it should not automatically be assumed all wealthy people send their children to private schools.

Perhaps one of the most important personal characteristics affecting consumer purchases, however, is an individual's personality. Personality refers to the behavioral and mental characteristics that distinguish an individual (Colman, 2006). These generally lead to consistent responses by individuals over time. There are any number of personality theories, many of which are rooted in the work of the Swiss personality theorist Carl Jung. Jung believed people have a predisposed, dominant personality tendency that guides their thoughts and behaviors (Bell, 1999). In his 1921 book *Psychological Type*, Jung proposed two attitudes: extroversion and introversion, along with four functions: sensation, intuition, thinking, and feeling (Jung, 1971). Jung's theory has served as the foundation for a number of personality indicators, including Myers-Briggs, Kiersey Temperament Sorter, and many others. Typically personalities are described in terms of traits, such as self-confidence, gregarious, or vengeful. For marketers, personality is especially important because, like a person, a brand can also have a personality. People tend to consume products and services reflecting their own personality or self-concept. As Mindset Media CEO Jim Meyer states, "Your personality determines what **you** consume, what TV shows **you watch**, what products **you** buy, and all the other decisions **you** make, political choices, for example" (Bulik, 2010).

External factors, such as culture, sub-culture, or social standing can also affect an individual's purchasing behavior. Culture refers to the ideas, beliefs, customs, and values within a society (Colman, 2006). What humans learn comes not only from the family but also from the culture and times. Because of this, marketers are continually on the watch for cultural trends, so they can identify opportunities to satisfy consumers' needs and wants. Similarly, sub-cultures, such as race, ethnicity, religion, ability, or geographic background can affect consumer preferences. Examples range from observance of holiday traditions, to support for a particular sports team, and from preparing traditional ethnic foods, to wearing religious icons.

Other external variables affecting purchasing decisions include social standing, such as working class or upper class, as well as the role an individual plays in society. For example, due to his or her position, a superintendent may be more likely to receive invitations to civic events than a departmental secretary. However, beyond our role in society, there is another external factor that has considerable power over consumers' choices: reference groups. This term, first coined in 1942 by US sociologist Herbert Hiram, refers to any group an individual takes as a standard in adopting opinions, attitudes, or behaviors (Colman, 2006). Reference groups can take many forms. For example, if a new hire in a company aspires to move up in her career, she may take her reference cues from top management. The resulting behavior can manifest itself in a number of ways, from a manner of speech to style of dress (Solomon, 2004).

The complex interplay of internal and external factors has a tremendous affect on consumers and the purchases they make. With that foundation in place, this section discussed the process consumers go through when making a purchasing decision. The purchasing process for consumers is triggered when the consumer recognizes a gap in his current state of being and some desired condition. It is this deficiency that marketers call a Need or the state felt deprivation. Needs exist on a number of levels. One of the most widely accepted explanations of needs was provided by the psychologist Abraham Maslow, who proposed a hierarchy of biogenic and psychogenic needs (Maslow, 1970). According to Maslow, our most basic needs are of a physiological nature, including food, water, and sleep. Beyond that, there are needs for safety, such as shelter, security, and protection. Moving up the hierarchy, the third level is for affiliation or belonging. This includes love, friendship, and acceptance. The fourth level includes ego needs, such as prestige, status, or accomplishment. The highest level of needs relate to self-actualization. Here individuals seek self-fulfillment or life-enriching experiences.

Consumers have a variety of different options available to satisfy their needs. How an individual wishes to satisfy his need is referred to as a Want. To distinguish Needs from Wants, consider that an individual is hungry, a need for food. How he desires to satisfy his hunger is shaped by individual personality and culture—those internal and external factors reviewed at the beginning of this section. For example, he may have a frugal personality (an internal psychological factor) and will happily settle for a simple ham sandwich. Conversely, he may want lobster and champagne because he has seen rich people in the movies (an external reference group factor) enjoying such delicacies.

It is this recognition of a Need within a consumer that is referred to as the Problem Recognition Stage in the Consumer Decision Process. This phase can occur for a number of reasons, such as running out of or breaking a product, or desiring a higher quality or status of living. The Problem Recognition period prompts the Information Search, or step two in the process. Here, consumers review a wide variety of information from two sources: internal and external. Internally, consumers will recall information from past purchases, advertisements, conversations with friends or co-workers, and the like. Externally, consumers will seek additional stimuli to reinforce or supplement their

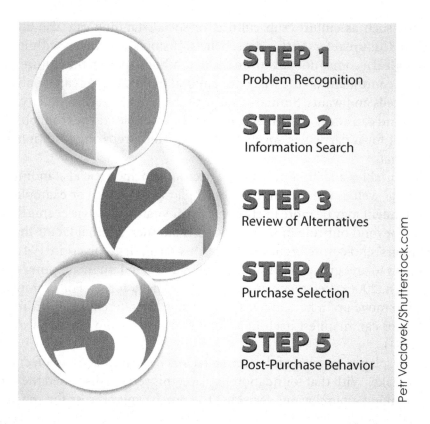

STEP 1
Problem Recognition

STEP 2
Information Search

STEP 3
Review of Alternatives

STEP 4
Purchase Selection

STEP 5
Post-Purchase Behavior

Petr Vaclavek/Shutterstock.com

internal memory. Sources here can include new advertisements, product articles or website searches, conversations with product sales representatives, and so forth.

The next stage involves the Evaluation of Alternatives, wherein consumers consider the brands they may or may not purchase. This is followed by the Product Choice step, when the consumer makes a selection based upon a set of criteria that help differentiate the various alternatives. The process concludes with some sort of Post-Purchase Behavior, typically characterized by the level of satisfaction the consumer experiences with the resulting outcome. It is at this point when the consumer may realize the decision made did not completely meet his needs. If this happens, the consumer enters a state of cognitive dissonance, or mental discord. Sometimes consumers will seek to internally resolve this conflict, perhaps by rationalizing some of the positive aspects tied to the decision, as a means of compensating for the negative consequences. This could include justifying the purchase by stating, "Well, this new car may not get the best gas mileage, but at least I didn't pay a fortune for it." Conversely, often Buyers will speak out and share their dissatisfaction—either with others or with the Seller. Recognizing that, at this stage, consumers can generate negative word-of-mouth attention about a brand, many companies—especially those selling products or services that represent a major investment—have put in place programs to follow up with Buyers after the purchase, to ensure their satisfaction or to rectify the problem. Examples include follow-up calls or post-purchase satisfaction surveys. In many private schools, new parent coffees or one-on-one interviews are commonly conducted, giving parents the opportunity to share questions or concerns, and the school the opportunity to address problems or reinforce parents' school selection decision.

Accompanying the Consumer Purchasing Decision Process, researchers have long appreciated a continuum distinguishing the level of effort and thought that go into a consumer's buying behavior. The graphic below illustrates the range of effort that typifies the various purchases consumers

FIGURE 2.1—Continuum of Buying Decision Behavior

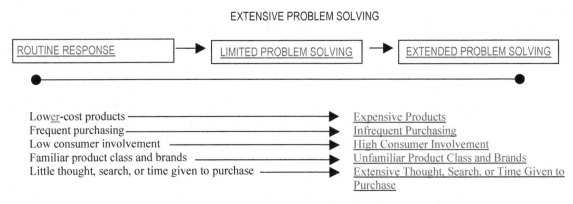

Adapted from Solomon, *Consumer Behavior: Buying, Having, and Being*, 9th ed., 2011.

make (Solomon, 2004). At the lower end of the spectrum, consumer effort is minimal, as a result of frequently repeated purchases involving low risk. In the mid-range, consumers expend a limited amount of effort, such as comparing brands, prices, styles, and the like, before making a purchase. While not routine, these mid-level purchases involve a more meaningful dollar figure, somewhat higher risk, which could include both financial and/or social (such as buying an unflattering pair of jeans), and may or may not have been made previously. The higher end of the continuum involves extensive effort on the consumer's part, involving infrequently made and higher risk purchases, such as a house, major appliance, or car.

Bildagentur Zoonar GmbH/Shutterstock.com

It should also be noted that consumers are not rational beings and they can very often be lazy in their decision-making as noted above about parents not making choices about schools. It is these quirks of human behavior that can result in either emotional or hasty decisions. Emotions cause humans to make a variety of unexplainable choices and purchases are no different. Recognizing this, marketers have used a number of advertising or selling techniques to successfully appeal to consumers' emotions. Beyond emotions, though, consumers do not always put forth the cognitive effort needed to engage in each step of the Purchase Decision Process. Very often they make immediate, rash decisions, a process known as heuristics. In his 2005 book *Blink, The Power of Thinking Without Thinking* (Gladwell, 2005), Malcolm Gladwell asserts his theory of rapid cognition, which he says is based on the brain's adaptive unconscious, "A kind of giant computer that quickly and quietly processes a lot of the data we need in order to keep functioning as human beings" (p. 11). The adaptive unconscious accounts for the brain's ability to make decisions quickly, and with very little information. The author presents repeated examples of this kind of spontaneous thinking. He uses the term "thin slicing" to refer to "the ability of our unconscious to find patterns in situations and behavior, based on very narrow slices of experiences" (p. 23).

A classic example of thin slicing is the experiences of many college-bound juniors and seniors. Even though the college or university they visited looked great on paper, has a wonderful website, prospective students when visiting make their decision in a matter of minutes. There may be something about how the other students are dressed, the cars in the parking lot may not be the right type, the town seems to have an odor. Many parents are often wondering what it is and what can be done to prevent long trips that prove unsuccessful.

Researchers have identified a number of short-cut decision rules Buyers use to weigh the various features or variables (both pro and con) tied to a particular purchase. With Noncompensatory Decision Rules, consumers eliminate all choices that do not comply with some basic standard (Solomon, 2004). For example, some Buyers insist on having their prescriptions filled with brand name medicines, never generic. Compensatory Decision Rules, on the other hand, are used when consumers are more involved with or invested in the purchasing decision and are willing to extend the cognitive effort necessary to make a good decision. In these cases, consumers contemplate both the positive and negative consequences tied to a particular purchase and select the option with the most positively weighted attributes.

Recognizing the intricacies of the purchasing decision-making process, many marketers have put in place programs to assist Buyers in making a decision which will successfully meet the consumers' needs. One example can be found in the diamond jewelry category. Here, marketers educate first-time diamond buyers of the four C's (color, cut, clarity, carat weight) to enable them to make informed purchasing decisions.

The next section focuses on market research resources marketers use to gain additional insights into consumer behavior. It will follow up by reviewing many of the characteristics surrounding the selection of a school and offer suggestions on steps public schools can take to play a more significant role in the Educational Consumer's purchasing decision.

Market Research

As discussed, the marketing planning process calls for marketers to make numerous decisions about consumers' likes, behaviors, and preferences. To better understand the specific attitudes, tastes, or purchasing intentions of consumers, marketers turn to a variety of market research resources to enable them to make more informed decisions related to the Marketing Mix. Research provides the kind of insights that helps organizations design products that meet consumers' needs, produce the quantity that will be demanded in the marketplace, assign a price point that will be attractive to Buyers, and develop a promotional messaging and media strategy that will motivate people to make a purchase. This section will review the Marketing Research process and provide resources and suggestions public school administrators can use to make effective marketing-related decisions.

Regardless of the size of the organization, managers need to make informed decisions related to the Marketing Mix. The Marketing Information System refers to the process managers use to obtain customer and market insights (Armstrong & Kotler, 2013). This system provides a structure for identifying information needs, gathering the necessary data, analyzing it, and reporting the findings back to management. Components of a Marketing Information System include internal databases, such as accounting records, sales figures, customer databases, advertising expenditures, or any other data that may help identify patterns or trends relative to business operations. Likewise, organizations utilize external data sources to provide information about competitors, customers, markets, or any other economic or cultural trends that may affect the organization. Finally, a Marketing Information System should also have the people and systems to support an organization's need to conduct its own original research.

The marketing research process begins by defining the research problem and then establishing the research objectives. The research problem relates to the root question the organization is trying to answer, while the research objectives seek to translate the problem into components or variables that can be investigated. From there, the organization must develop a research plan for collecting the necessary information, which can include both primary and secondary research. Step three in the process involves the actual implementation of the research plan—specifically, the collection and analysis of the data. Finally, the data must be interpreted and the findings reported.

Secondary Research

Secondary research includes a wide variety of information that already exists, having been collected for some other purpose. Sources for secondary information can come through a variety of channels, including library databases, industry trade associations, government data, and competitor websites. These internal and external sources are generally referred to as secondary data—information gathered for some other purpose, but which may prove useful for the decision at hand (Churchill, 1991). These secondary sources can assist astute, insightful marketing decision makers in much the same way that a literature review guides a scholarly thesis or dissertation research inquiry. Furthermore, the ready availability of secondary research can help save valuable time and resources for managers looking to obtain information quickly and inexpensively. Though secondary sources may not provide the answers for every management question, they can make a primary research investigation more productive, by helping frame questions or direct the focus of a research question.

Sources of secondary research, which may prove useful to public school educators, are shown in Table 2.1. These resources will help educators answer questions related to the demographic, economic, or lifestyle of potential educational consumers.

TABLE 2.1—Secondary Research Sources for Educators

Source	Description	Website Link
NAICS Association (North American Industry Classification System)	Offers research and other information related to specific industries. Other services include marketing and customer lists.	http://www.naics.com/
US Census NAICS data	Use the Data tab to find a variety of information, such as population data, economic census information, maps, statistics, catalogs, and a lot more.	http://www.census.gov/eos/www/naics/
US Economic Census	Results of an economic census conducted every five years, providing US National and local economies.	http://www.census.gov/econ/census07/
Encyclopedia of American Industries	SIC 9411—Administration of Educational Programs.	http://www.referenceforbusiness.com/industries/Public-Administration/Administration-Educational-Programs.html
Encyclopedia of Associations	Source for detailed information on associations, worldwide (including Education)	http://find.galegroup.com/gdl/help/GDLeDirEAHelp.html
Reference USA	Reference database for business and consumer research. NOTE: some libraries can provide access to this source.	http://www.referenceusa.com/
Infoplease	Searchable database providing fast information on a variety of topics.	http://www.infoplease.com/
Neilsen Zip Code Look-up	Provides lifestyle information for Zip Codes, using the Neilsen Prizm segmentation system. Quick facts include population, age, income, and median household spending data.	http://www.claritas.com/MyBestSegments/Default.jsp?ID=20&SubID=&pageName=ZIP%2BCode%2BLook-up
US Bureau of Labor Statistics	Offers a number of subject area reports, databases, and tools. For example, Consumer Expenditure, and Time Usage surveys. Other tools help simplify the data access and use process.	http://www.bls.gov/data/

Source	Description	Website Link
US Government Bookstore	Clearinghouse of free or inexpensive government ebooks, books, and subscription publication. Search Education to see more than 80 publication results.	http://bookstore.gpo.gov/index.jsp
Market Research World	A portal for online resources for market research. Search the Education Training sector.	http://www.marketresearchworld.net/content/category/8/51/77/
DJS Research`	Education Market Research Insights and Findings database.	http://www.djsresearch.co.uk/EducationMarketResearchInsightsAndFindings/articles
Wolfram Alpha	Offering unique solutions to finding and using information covering a wide range of areas, including education. Some information is free, subscriptions to Wolfram Alpha area also available. (Educational pricing discounts offered.)	http://www.wolframalpha.com/examples/
Education Market Research	Offering K–12 marketing research on a wide variety of topics. Some reports paid, but other resources are free.	http://www.educationmarketresearch.com/
IBIS World	Public Schools in the US: Market Research Report. Offering industry insights, statistics, analysis and trends. Free snapshot information and sample reports offered, along with a variety of purchase options available.	http://www.ibisworld.com/industry/default.aspx?indid=1940

Primary Research

To the extent that secondary sources alone are not sufficient enough to provide the necessary information to meet management's decision-making needs, primary research can be used. Since it is quite likely most educators will be familiar with the traditional research process, this section will provide a brief summary of various types of research methods and then offer additional resources that public school educators can use to conduct their own primary investigations. Research for gathering primary data includes observations, focus groups, experiments, and surveys (Kotler & Keller, 2012).

Observational research involves watching the situation, individual, or group of interest and recording relevant facts, actions, or behaviors (Churchill, 1991). Methods of collecting observational data can include in-person observations and interviews, mechanical data collection—such as attendance counters, audio or videotaping, and ethnographies. Ethnographic research incorporates a wide variety of techniques where researchers observe or interact with subjects in their natural environments.

Focus group research uses a small group of 6–10 individuals (identified on the basis of some qualifying characteristic) to talk about a product, service, issue, or organization. Led by a trained moderator, the purpose of the discussion is not to arrive at a consensus or conclusion, but rather to gain insights or opinions related to the topic of discussion.

Experimental research uses groups of subjects and then applies different treatments—manipulating one variable for the test group, while holding the same variable constant for the control group and then comparing the results by checking for different outcomes or responses between the groups. Experiments are used to explain cause–effect relationships. An example of a simple marketing research experiment could entail exposing subject groups to different advertising messages for the same product and then measuring the effects with sales or memory recall.

Survey research allows researchers to gather primary data by asking questions about knowledge, attitudes, preferences, and buying behavior. It is probably one of the most widely used forms of primary data collection. In addition, there are a number of different options available to researchers who wish to collect data through a survey questionnaire. These include mail, telephone, face-to-face, and online. While each of these communication options has its own set of strengths, weaknesses, and costs, the flexibility of collecting data in this manner is why surveys remain the most popular data collection tool.

Beyond data collection methods, there are a number of other considerations for marketers wishing to undertake a primary investigation. While the entire marketing research process will not be reviewed in this section, it will identify two additional factors that must be taken into account when conducting a primary investigation. The first relates to population measurement. Two options exist; they include doing a census or using a sample. A census seeks to measure all the members of the population being examined. For a large population, this is an especially difficult task. In fact, while attempting to measure all citizens, the US Census does not actually count every person in the country. For example, lower-income and rural areas present tremendous difficulties for census workers to reach by way of mail or door-to-door contact methods (The Leadership Conference, 2013). However, by its own defined goal to measure 100% of the population, census data (if achieved) is 100% accurate. Therefore, for investigations involving extremely small populations, a census is always recommended.

However, because a census is difficult to implement, researchers often use sample sizes to measure the attitudes, opinions, or behaviors of a large population. A sample examines a carefully chosen segment of the population, to represent the entire population. Important considerations here involve selecting the sample using either probability or nonprobability sampling techniques. A probability sample is one in which each member of the population has an equal chance of being included in the sample (Churchill, 1991). A nonprobability sample relies on judgment or other selection methods that prohibit the statistical calculation of a population member's chances of being included in the sample. Having said that, though, many researchers use nonprobability data collection methods, such as convenience, judgment, and quota sampling in an attempt to fully and accurately represent the range of members found within the population being assessed.

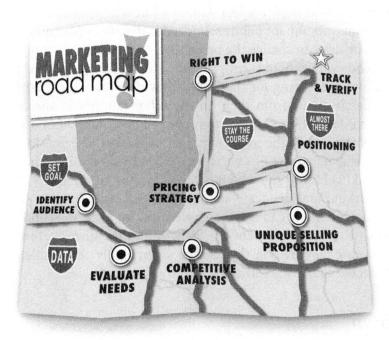

The second consideration for market researchers relates to the measurement scales used in the data collection instrument. Again, without going into a long diatribe on questionnaire design, what is most important is to know the measurement scale being used is a valid one, meaning it measures what it is supposed to gauge. To appreciate this, consider using a weight scale to measure a person's age or a calendar to determine an individual's height. While that sounds crazy, consider further how difficult it is to measure elements of a nonphysical nature, such as attitudes or opinions, and how easy it would be to do it incorrectly. However, these later variables are very often what marketers are most interested in examining. Many people who design a survey think they know what they want to ask, so they simply compile a list of questions and put them on the questionnaire, giving little or no consideration to the validity or accuracy of the instrument they have created. With this in mind, public school administrators should examine any number of marketing-related variables to use measurement scales that have already been verified. Perhaps the best collection of marketing scales is found in the resource published by Gordon Bruner II, *Marketing Scales Handbook* (Bruner, 2013). This book provides reviews of scales along with the empirical evidence that supports their quality. Many of these scales are adaptable to a wide range of topics.

Understanding consumers isn't easy or simple. There are a number of issues marketers must consider when attempting to understand the target population to which they hope to market their product. When collected properly and used effectively, marketing research can help minimize the guesswork in making important marketing decisions. The next section applies these concepts to the public school setting.

Analyzing the Needs of Your Families, Students, and Community

As has been pointed out, public education historically had a monopoly on the provision of educational services for the students who lived in their district. They often did little more than monitor the number of students in each grade, count the new students, or incoming kindergarten class, and then plan based solely on that number. With new choices, families can now choose to send their children to other schools. The important question for public school educators is to determine why that choice was made, and then what can be done to change the perception of their public school system.

Researching who attends your school is simple. They are a captive audience. Families have made a choice for their child and are hoping for the best. Knowing whom these families are is the easy part. One can make generalizations from them to the other families in the community, but that won't necessarily give the information required to really tell how the school district is doing in the community and how it is perceived. The important part of market research for public education is to really answer the basic research questions necessary: (1) Why do families choose the schools they send their children to? and (2) How is the school perceived in the community? Answering these two questions will help understand and delineate any necessary changes that can and should be made to help market your school. Teachers can ask these questions on back-to-school nights, as a part of kindergarten screenings, or for a new student who moves into the district. Teachers can be a great source of information because they are non-threatening, often highly personable, and can and should be used as a great and reliable source for gathering information.

Informal Research

The easiest form of market research for educators is informal. Informal research entails asking others about their perceptions of the school. It may have a directive to answer how people perceive what is going on, but it may be also used to help determine research objectives as to why people are making the choices they are making (Frameworks, 2002). There is no specific set of questions addressed. The comments from the others steer the conversation, and there is no formal analysis of the information to help determine trends and needs. Many educators are doing informal research all the time, without even realizing it. This is information gathering that comes from talking with others and just listening to why they make the choices they make, and listening to them about their perceptions of the schools.

Informal research is easy and it is (hopefully) done all the time. It is anecdotal and relies on others (Timm & Farr, 1994). This is typically done by just overhearing others in conversations, reading letters to the editor about the concerns presented, talking with business leaders about their needs and observations, and asking high school students who are at private schools about why they made the choice they did. Listening as people present their concerns about the schools is a very valuable part of any educator's job. For many educators, this is the only method they use to gather information about what needs to be done to help change or improve the services they provide (Lunenberg & Ornstein, 2011). As noted above, teachers have a "gut reaction" for the parents and others that they talk with. Use this information. It is real, invaluable, and could help make a very different future for your public school.

The informal method is great for basic information gathering. It is also a great and time-honored way for the public to communicate with the educators in the public school. It brings to the forefront the important questions and problems others have about what is going on with their schools. Not addressing (or at least considering) these concerns can cause irreparable perception problems with the educators as being out of touch and not listening to the taxpayers.

While informal research is good, there are some inherent biases presented that may give the indication that public school employees really have a feel for what is going on in the district and is addressing the needs. When public school employees rely on informal research such as described above, they are addressing the needs of their friends, their friend's friends, and the vocal minority that seeks to be heard. It also falls prey to the whims and desires of the actions of the public school employee's interests. If a principal or teacher is very interested in the marching band (because of

Roobcio/Shutterstock.com

previous involvement or having a child in the marching band), there will be much discussion of the needs of the marching band relating to uniforms, travel, expenses, and practice sessions. The needs of the marching band may be completely valid and there may be needs that really need to be addressed. But, the needs of the members of the cross-country team may be neglected because the teacher is spending all of his or her time with the parents of the marching band. Spending a lot of time with one group can lead to a neglect of the needs of another group.

Again, the need of the marching band may be important, but administrators have a responsibility to address the needs of <u>all</u> the students in the school, not just the ones from which they hear. However, an administrator may believe that, since the marching band gets a lot of attention in the newspaper, the school is getting all the positive press it needs, and that marketing research is not needed. Do administrators really know how their schools are perceived in the community? Do they know how the parents of the debate team feel? Do they know the attitudes of the parents of the students in vocational education? Do they know the attitudes of the parents of second-graders? Do they know the attitudes of parents with a child in special education? What about the teachers? Are they all happy or at least content with how they are treated and the work assigned to them?

Formal Research

As we have stated, the purpose of this book is to give tips and advice to public school employees to help them develop a plan for marketing their school. The problem is many public school educators view the ideas espoused in this book as time-consuming and not worth the effort. However, making decisions based on the knowledge that comes solely from informal marketing can waste time and resources, exacerbate problems with groups that are not normally vocal about problems, and cause very real needs of students to go unmet. There is also a fear factor associated with doing more formal market research. One may find the reason families choose to send their child to a private school is based on the perceived incompetence of the educators in the public school.

The first step for educators in formal marketing research is to identify the target population. Most likely your target population will be the families of school age children living in the geographical boundary of the district. For others, it may be the attitudes and perceptions of the business leaders and what they think about the education the students are receiving.

It is vital to accurately identify the target population and then develop a plan for how to get the information needed. This sounds easy, but requires asking questions one may or may not want to hear answered. It also requires establishing a formal process of obtaining the information and then synthesizing it with current practices. The steps in a formal educational marketing research plan are:

1. Objective of research
2. How to get information
3. Actual collection of information
4. Analysis and Response to the findings

It is imperative to view taking data on the goals and objectives of the school as a rolling target, similar to how political campaigns continually survey possible voters to see if there are changes. Another important point is that step four could be viewed as the most important in the process. Many educators know (with great pain) there are many reports or descriptive papers written that then sit on a shelf without any hope of either being read or being implemented. Therefore, using the information gathered and making sure the people who helped gather the data are aware of how to implement it is extremely important. Finally, if as a result of the gathering of information one learns of a need that will be expensive, try to determine potential support for the new findings.

Step One: Objectives of Research

When looking at the goal of market research for public schools, there does not have to be one overarching question; multiple questions should be addressed depending on the presented needs. The hard part about the establishment of a research agenda is determining what is unknown. As noted above, educators make a lot of assumptions based on the informal research about what is known. However, it is often anecdotal and dependent upon casual conversations with people public school employees contact.

The following is not meant to be a definitive list, but to be used to help tailor a marketing effort in a local school district. It starts with surveying the population already in the district (parents and students who are currently enrolled), and moves out to parents and students who are not enrolled in the district. It will involve work, but it will help any administrator to better understand the role their district plays in the local community. It will also be important to share with school board members to help explain the direction the district is taking as a part of the education of all students.

It is important to start with the individuals already committed to the public school, through either attendance or employment, because as will be demonstrated later, these individuals will often be the most important marketers of any public school. If they are not happy, they will share with others the concerns and may cause some parents to enroll their children in different schools (or move to a different school themselves). The important points raised by the individuals already involved in your school need to be addressed so that can be conveyed to the public. Starting with Who Attends and/or Works in the School:

1. How satisfied are the students?
2. How satisfied are the employees?
3. How satisfied are the volunteers?
4. How satisfied are the parents of the students enrolled?
5. What are some of the most important concerns of the students?
6. What are some of the most important concerns of the employees?

7. What are some of the important concerns of the volunteers?
8. What are some of the important concerns of the parents?
9. How do you get information about the schools in the area?
10. How do you perceive the public school in your area?

Again, using the information generated by the individuals already involved with the school to gain a clearer idea of their feelings is an important step. Also, making sure the information gathered from them is used to help improve the school environment is vital. In the end, these individuals will be your best marketers. They do not, however, tell the whole story of the perception of the public school in the community.

From a legal perspective there may be rules in your states about surveying students about their attitudes and feeling about the schools. Be sure to check with your school district solicitor before moving forward in this area just to make sure.

Just like after each election, a losing campaign should conduct a post-mortem about what worked and what should have changed, and try to determine why individuals did not vote for a specific candidate; public schools need to think in a similar vein. This will take a lot more work to do, because individuals not currently involved with the public schools will have to be found and they will need to be willing to give up some time talking about a subject that does not typically involve them. However, this will probably be some of the most valuable information you will get as a part of the development of a marketing plan for public schools.

This book is designed to help public schools address the dwindling market share they currently have, and then to find ways of getting an accurate description of the services they provide to the community as a whole, so parents can make an informed decision. The following questions are for those families not currently involved in the public school system. When addressing them, a good public school educator will understand more about the decision making process of the families who choose to send their children elsewhere, where they get their information, and their main competitors. First, the questions and then suggestions about how to get answers:

1. Why did you choose not to send your child to the public schools?
2. How do you get information about the schools in the area?
3. What are you looking for in a school?
4. How do you perceive the public school in your area?
5. Where do you send your children to school?

Steps Two and Three: How to Get Information and Actual Collection of the Information

Given the questions—to both individuals involved with the public schools and those who are not—how does one obtain the answers from both of these groups? There are many books on research and eliciting responses from individuals as a part of a marketing plan. It is beyond the scope of this book to go into the level of detail in describing how to do those. Some of the books and websites that have great descriptions of these methods for marketing research include:

Focus Groups

Krueger, R. A., & Casey, M. A. (2008). *Focus groups: A practical guide for applied research (4th ed.).* Thousand Oaks, CA: Sage Publications.

Rubin, H. J., & Rubin, I. S. (2011). *Qualitative interviewing: The art of hearing data.* Thousand Oaks, CA: Sage Publications.

Survey Research

Henry, P. H., Lipsey, M. W., & Freeman, H. E. (2003). *Evaluation: A systematic approach (7th ed)*. Thousand Oaks, CA: Sage Publications.

Websites
Survey Research

1. http://www.socialresearchmethods.net/kb/survey.php
2. http://writing.colostate.edu/guides/guide.cfm?guideid=68
3. http://csr.indiana.edu

Educators need to realize they do not have to go it alone to get the work done, because as it is well known, the public school employee's job is full-time, be it an administrator or a teacher, and adding the requirements of researching the current employees, students, and members of the community as a whole can be overwhelming. A positive about hiring or contracting with an outside agency or university is this conveys to the participants a nonpartisan and more anonymous system that may help with the authenticity of responses.

There are local research and consulting firms that can help with market research, and grants may help pay for some of the necessary work. Another possible resource, one that is often looking for work, is that of local colleges and universities. Departments of educational leadership, marketing, political science, or social work, as well as MBA programs, at local colleges or universities can be invaluable resources and a supply of available student help who may be willing to work on a survey as a part of a class project. They would need to be overseen, and given clear guidance, but the possible production of viable and usable information from a student or class project should not be overlooked or discounted. These colleges and universities technically do not have to be that close geographically due to the wide use of Internet research.

Another possibility for research is a local chamber of commerce or small business development agency. They often do free assessments and surveys for businesses and can be approached about helping to determine attitudes and feelings about the local public schools as a part of business development.

What administrators need to realize in conducting marketing research is that, no matter what direction is chosen, there are pros and cons to each method. The following will help describe the basic functions of each of the various methods, with a brief example of how an educator might use the methods in his or her school district, with some of the pros and cons of the methods. The important part of the process is to remember the goals for the questions, to determine what others really think of the public schools and how they make the decision to send or not send their child to the school.

The main sources of gathering information include focus groups, written surveys, telephone surveys, and Internet surveys. Each has its own strengths and weaknesses, and each presents the information in a subtly different way. One is not inherently better than the others, and the choice of which to use may depend solely on the opportunity to have access to individuals to research. These methods can be used on the population already affiliated with the school as was discussed before, and can also be used with the population with no current ties to the local school district.

Focus groups were described elsewhere in this chapter. They are good because of the depth of information that may be obtained about the feelings these individuals have toward a public school. The disadvantage is the group may not be representative of the attitudes and beliefs of the groups educators are interested in. Also, the sheer volume of information presented in a focus group may make it difficult to understand what really is of concern to the group and what was just mentioned to fill time. Good focus group leaders, however, can work to effectively parse out the main attitudes from a group versus the ones that are not as important. One of the last disadvantages of focus groups is that they can cost a lot of money. Money is needed to pay the focus group leader, the costs of the observers, and the costs for any refreshments provided.

Surveys are another possible method of gathering information about the residents of the district and their views. They are typically systematic methods of gathering information from the residents of the district. There are different types of surveys, written, telephone, and online. Each have a unique place in the gathering of information, and a well-thought out survey can deliver valuable information to a school district. Surveys can also provide quantifiable information for a district for specific needs and services, and depending on the anonymity of the individual being surveyed, may provide information that other methods may not due to a fear of retribution or recrimination. There are also potential problems with the use of surveys including answering machines or lack of numbers for telephone surveys, and skewed results from only those with online access in Internet surveys. There is also the expected considerable amount of time spent in developing the right questions so everyone involved with the survey understands precisely what is being asked.

Step Four—Analysis and Response

This section depends on the questions you have asked and the information that has returned. Starting this process involves a commitment to use the information returned—both positive and negative—to help make informed decisions about future actions of the district. As noted above, reports written and then shelved provide little or no use for those in the district. It may frustrate the report writer and those who participated in the process. When asking questions painful truths (or opinions) may come out. Asking questions about employee or student satisfaction may uncover truths some administrators are unprepared to accept. Another important point about the various forms of market research is to make sure there is no hidden agenda. It is ineffective to seek out predetermined results. This will foster resentment and a lack of respect.

Using the research questions listed previously will help steer the agenda for the school. However, that should not be where the process ends. Informal research is an ongoing daily endeavor, providing benefits to those who the administrator regularly contacts. What also need to be addressed are the other individuals who do not talk with administrators and have serious problems with the public schools. As has been noted elsewhere, parents often make their decisions about which school their child will attend on longstanding opinions of what is perceived as good—but may not be. It is important to understand what parents feel is important in the decision-making process, understand the competition, but also understand the perceptions of the community about the school. Without that, public school educators cannot in good faith accurately state they truly know what is going on with their school.

Chapter 2—SPOTLIGHT: School Visit

The Pearson family had always enrolled their child in private schools. Both parents had also attended private schools, so they had very little familiarity with their local public school system, other than a general awareness that it was considered to be a "good school system." However, when the economy shifted, they began to look at their family finances and decided to investigate the possibility of transferring their child to the public school. In early October, Mrs. Pearson contacted the local middle school to arrange a shadow visit for her son Sean. She called several times and left numerous messages, which were never returned. At one point, she reached a receptionist who said the Principal's secretary was the person who arranged such visits. Over the next month, she left various messages for the secretary, which, again, were never returned. The holidays came and went and, once again, Mrs. Pearson attempted to contact the school to see if a visit for her son could be arranged. Finally, out of disgust, she called the school and asked to speak to the Principal, who was unavailable. Mrs. Pearson left a frank voice mail recounting her difficulty in scheduling a shadow date and asked the Principal to return the call. Within the hour, the Principal called and apologized and offered to arrange a visit. She asked probing questions about Sean, in terms of his likes and interests, so that she could pair him with a compatible shadow match. She assured Mrs. Pearson that she would personally greet them on the day of the arranged visit to introduce Sean to the student who would host the shadow.

On the day of the visit, Mrs. Pearson and Sean walked into the school's front hall and asked the receptionist if they could see the Principal. They were told she was in a meeting. The receptionist asked what they needed and was completely unaware of the pending visit. Flustered, she tried to cover, saying that *"the school did have shadow visits from time to time"* . . . *"perhaps there were two or three scheduled that day,"* . . . and she was sure *"they could figure something out."* Becoming quite nervous, Mrs. Pearson asked the receptionist if she wanted any emergency contact information, at which point the receptionist asked for Sean's name (which she misspelled three times) and the family's street address. Mrs. Pearson suggested it might be better if the receptionist took both parent's names and cell phone numbers, as opposed to a mailing address. At this point, Mrs. Pearson was quite unsettled, though she didn't want to alarm Sean, since she didn't want him to become upset about having to spend the day at an unknown (and unorganized) school. Finally, another office secretary who had been listening to the conversation related that the Principal didn't always share shadow information with the front office staff but that there probably was a shadow arranged, if they had shown up expecting one. Remembering all the trouble it took to arrange this visit, Mrs. Pearson decided to go ahead and let Sean complete the shadow day.

At the end of the school day, Mrs. Pearson picked up Sean. The Principal had in fact, arranged a shadow visit and the day went along fine. The boy Sean was paired with had similar interests in sports and, at lunch, Sean recognized a few other kids from church and little league. The receptionist wished them well as they walked out the door. That was the last they ever heard from the school.

Questions

1. Who are the educational consumers in this scenario?
2. What are the needs of the educational consumers in this scenario? Were they met?
3. Do you think the Pearsons will be enrolling Sean in the school?
4. What systems could the school put in place to address the issues addressed in this case?

Applying the Concepts

1. Who are your customers?
2. How are families treated when they come to visit your school for the first time?
3. Why do your students and families choose your school?
4. Why do students and families choose to leave your school?
5. Based on data and research efforts, what need does your school meet for your community?

References

Armstrong, G., & Kotler, P. (2013). *Marketing: An Introduction* (11th ed.). Boston, MA: Pearson.

Bell, A. (1999). *Psychological profiles: Personality tests can help you build a compatible work-group and learn more about yourself.* Retrieved from www.nwfusion.com

Bruner, II, G. (2013). *Marketing Scales Handbook. Vol. 5.* Retrieved from http://www.marketingscales.com/publications/marketing-scales-ebook-v5

Bukhari, P., & Randall, E. V. (2009). Exit and entry: Why parents in Utah left public schools and chose private schools. *Journal of School Choice, 3,* 242–270.

Bulik, B. S. (2010). You are what you watch, market data suggest. *Advertising Age 81*(39), 12. Retrieved from http://adage.com/article/news/research-links-personality-traits-tv-viewing-habits/146779/

Churchill, G. (1991). *Marketing Research Methodological Foundations* (5th ed.). Orlando, FL: Dryden Press.

Colman, A. (2006). *Oxford Dictionary of Psychology,* (2nd ed.). New York: Oxford University Press.

Council for American Private Education. (2013). *Choosing a school.* Retrieved from http://capenet.org/

Damron, M. (2012). *Indiana voucher program more than doubles enrollment. Indiana Department of Education.* Retrieved from http://www.doe.in.gov/news/indiana-voucher-program-more-doubles-enrollment

Davis, H. (1972). Decision making within the household. *Journal of Consumer Research, 2* (March, 1982), 241–260.

Doyle, M. C., & Feldman, J. (2006). Student voice and school choice in the Boston Pilot High Schools. *Educational Policy, 20*(2), 367–398.

Foxman, E. Tansuhaj, P. and Ekstrom, K. (1989). Family members' perceptions of adolescents' influence in family decision making. *Journal of Consumer Research 15* (4), 482-491.

Frameworks Institute (2002). Framing public issues. Washington, DC: Frameworks Institute.

Freidman Foundation. (2013). *The ABCs of School Choice. The Friedman Foundation for Educational Choice.* Retrieved from www.edchoice.org

Gladwell, M. (2005). *Blink. The Power of Thinking Without Thinking.* New York: Back Bay Books/Little, Brown and Company/Hachette Book Group USA.

Jung, C. G. ([1921] 1971). *Psychological Types, Collected Works, Volume 6.* Princeton, NJ: Princeton University Press.

Kotler, P., & Keller, K. (2012). *Marketing Management* (14th ed.). Upper Saddle River, NJ: Pearson Education.

The Leadership Conference. (2013). *Reasons behind inaccuracies in the Census.* Retrieved from www.civilrights.org/census/accurate-count/inaccuracies.html

Lunenberg, F. C., & Ornstein, A. C. (2011). Educational administration: *Concepts and practices.* Boston: Wadsworth Publishing.

Maslow, A. H. (1970). *Motivation and Personality* (2nd ed.). New York: Harper & Row.

National Alliance for Public Charter Schools (NAPCS). (2013). *Public charter schools today.* Retrieved from http://www.publiccharters.org National Alliance for Public Charter Schools.

National Center of Education Statistics. (2010). *Trends in the use of school choice: 1997–2007.* Retrieved from http://nces.ed.gov/pubs2010/2010004/

National Home Education Research Institute. (2013). *Reasons parents choose to home school.* Retrieved from http://www.nheri.org/

Nichols, M. P., & Schwartz, R. C. (1994). *Family therapy* (3rd ed.). Boston: Allyn & Bacon.

Seymour, D., & Lessne, G. Spousal conflict arousal: Scale development. *Journal of Consumer Research 11*(3). 810–821.

Solomon, M. R. (2004). *Consumer Behavior—Buying, Having and Being* (6th ed.). Upper Saddle River, NJ: Pearson Prentice Hall.

Thomson, E., Laing, A., & McKee, L. (2007). Family purchase decision making: Exploring child influence behavior. *Journal of Consumer Behavior 6*(4). 182–202.

Timm, P. R., & Farr, R. C. (1994). *Business research.* Seattle: Crisp Publications.

Wolf, P. J. (2012). *The comprehensive longitudinal evaluation of the Milwaukee Parental Choice Program: Summary of the Final Report.* Fayetteville, AR: Department of Education Reform, School Choice Demonstration Project, University of Arkansas.

Wolf, P. J., Gutmann, B., Pums, M., Kisida, B., Rizzo, L., Eissa, N., & Carr, M. (2010). *Evaluation of the DC Opportunity Scholarship Program: Final Report.* Fayetteville, AR: Department of Education Reform, School Choice Demonstration Project, University of Arkansas.

Wolf, P. J., & Stewart, T. (2012). *Understanding School Shoppers in Detroit.* Fayetteville, AR: Department of Education Reform, School Choice Demonstration Project, University of Arkansas.

Chapter 3

Strategic Marketing Planning

Marketing is so basic that it cannot be considered a separate function within the business. . . . But it is, first, a central dimension of the entire business.

–Peter Drucker, Founder of Modern Management Practices

The billboard on the highway outside of a large city in the southeast of the US advertises a private school with the slogan:

Preparing for College: Preparing for Life.

xtock/Shutterstock.com

He finally had time to develop a marketing plan.

The Internet ads say the same thing. The secretary answers the phone with that. When you are put on hold, you hear a description of that slogan and get directed to the school's web page which greets you with that slogan again, and there are numerous rotating pictures of students in libraries, science labs, and in front of computers—all happy, but serious. All of these images and the constant use of the phrase convey an understanding that these students are preparing for college—and for life. The phrase and advertising are ubiquitous. People who have never had children describe the school as a good place to prepare for college.

How did that school come to market itself like this?

Within organizations, the Marketing function plays a pivotal role. Marketing participates in the development of corporate strategies and assists in the planning, implementation, and evaluation of those strategies. The manner in which the marketing function is structured is highly dependent on the size and scope of the organization. For example, large corporations with many business units will have a correspondingly large marketing division, while the owner himself may make the marketing decisions for a small business. In this chapter, we will review the marketing process and discuss practical ways in which the marketing process can be incorporated into a public school setting. The strategic marketing process can be broken out into four distinct steps: Analysis, Planning, Implementation, and Evaluation/Control (Cravens, 1994).

Marketing Analysis and Planning

Before a marketing strategy can be pursued, an analysis of the markets to be served must first be completed. A Market is defined as the set of all actual and potential buyers of a product or service (Armstrong & Kotler, 2013). As we reviewed in Chapter One, the Marketing Analysis process entails four main steps: Segmentation, Target Market Selection, Marketing Strategy, and Positioning. Other aspects of the situation analysis process include gathering marketing intelligence, which was reviewed in Chapter Two. Once the analysis phase has been completed, the organization is ready to focus more specifically on planning each component of the marketing mix.

As we have stated, the Marketing Mix includes Product, Price, Place, and Promotion. The term was first coined in 1964 by Harvard marketing professor Neil Borden, who credited Professor James Culliton with describing the marketing executive as a "mixer of ingredients" (Borden, 1984, p. 7). As Borden explains, the competitive and environmental circumstances facing an organization are ever-changing. Management can respond in a number of ways, including developing products, expanding distribution outlets, changing pricing procedures, or utilizing aggressive promotions. While these may be day-to-day responses, the overall strategy represents the organization's Marketing Mix.

Strategic planning for products or services encompasses three areas: planning for new products, managing strategies for existing successful products, and developing programs for unsuccessful products (Cravens, 1994). Organizations must put in place systems for gauging a product's performance. Performance can be measured in both a financial and nonfinancial manner. Financial metrics include revenues, costs, and profit. Nonfinancial assessments include such things as customer awareness and satisfaction measurements. From a marketing perspective, financial measurements that make sense for schools include enrollment and costs. From a nonfinancial standpoint, there are many measures a school could use to its competitive advantage— parental satisfaction survey results, test scores, college placement and scholarship statistics, to name only a few.

Strategic planning decisions for product distribution must be consistent with the product and its positioning. A good distribution network can actually create a competitive advantage for a brand. Organizations must be able to deliver the product in a manner that meets customers' needs. Traditional businesses have a number of logistical issues to plan for—such as transportation, warehousing, inventory, and order processing. In addition, businesses must consider whether their distribution network will incorporate traditional brick-and-mortar locations, utilize a virtual e-commerce platform—or a combination of both. For schools, these same options are now available.

Where pricing is concerned, product managers must plan an effective strategy for the brand. In general, a product's price quantifies the value of the exchange. Where complex purchases are concerned, price is considered synonymous with quality (Cravens, 1994). A company can employ any number of pricing strategies to achieve a particular objective. For example, a low-price strategy can be used to increase market share, stimulate demand, or respond to competition. Effective pricing strategies can also be used to help a company improve financial performance or establish its product positioning. Chapter Six addresses the unique circumstances that surround "pricing decisions" for public schools.

Promotion strategy combines advertising, personal selling, sales promotion, and public relations. Often referred to as the Promotion Mix, these tools can dramatically influence an organization's ability to successfully influence consumer decision-making. Selection of the appropriate promotional tools must take into consideration the specific marketing objective the organization wishes to achieve. Further, because the promotional mix represents significant costs, organizations must identify the manner in which the promotional budget will be established.

Organizations typically utilize one of four methods for setting the promotional budget (Kotler & Keller, 2012). The first budgeting method uses a Percent of Sales. Employed by organizations with a good sense of their sales history and reliable sales forecasting methods, this approach sets a fixed percentage of sales, such as 10%, to use as the marketing budget moving forward. While this method is popular with many industries, it tends to ignore sales cycles and can lead to over-promotion in periods when sales are naturally slow, or under-promotion in a competitive selling environment.

The second method, Competitive Parity, is tied to the spending levels of competitors. However, this method ignores the differences that exist between competitors and the marketing strategies being pursued. The third approach to setting a promotional budget recognizes the financial limitations that exist in many organizations, especially small businesses. Called simply the All You Can Afford method, the business sets aside for promotion an amount that can fit within the overall operating budget. The final method is referred to as Objective and Task. This method outlines communication objectives and the tasks necessary to achieve them. From there, the costs associated with each task are calculated. This approach to budgeting is the most logical and widely used method.

The marketing planning process, while detailed and time-consuming, forces organizations to consider all decisions related to the Marketing Mix, prior to jumping in blindly. Such forethought allows organizations to contemplate the consequences the planned Marketing Mix efforts will have on the organization, in terms of costs, revenues, timetable, and competitive reactions, to name just a few variables. Most organizations establish annual marketing plans and update that plan quarterly, to allow for adjustments based on developing challenges or opportunities. The components of a marketing plan, as recommended by the American Marketing Association, are provided in Chapter 9. However, regardless of how detailed a plan the organization develops, the key components of a marketing plan include the situation analysis and the marketing plan (Lehmann & Winer, 1991). The situation analysis addresses the economic and business environment in which the organization is operating, along with the problems or opportunities currently being faced. The marketing plan outlines the strategies the organization hopes to achieve within the time period of the plan, along with the products or services that will be sold, the customers being pursued, the competition, and the specific tactics that will be undertaken—broken out by product, price, place, and promotion. The marketing plan will also include any relevant research supporting the proposed marketing plan actions, along with the key financial documentation—the marketing budget and a profit/loss statement.

For non-business organizations looking to adopt a marketing orientation, the best way to begin is to appoint a marketing committee charged with identifying the problems and opportunities facing the organization (Kotler, 1988). Beyond that, the committee should consider what type of marketing function would fit within the institutional framework and whether or not there is a need for a full-time marketing manager or staff. In the next section, we will discuss ways public schools can adopt a marketing orientation.

We are making some assumptions that as a public school employee reading this book you are concerned with how to market your school better. You realize things need to change to improve your school's marketing efforts, and hopefully you have learned from the first two chapters that educational marketing is more than just telling your story. It is a whole concerted effort or research, analysis, and then implementation.

First, analysis. Determining the need for a marketing orientation for schools is a great place to start. Why are you considering this? Are other schools taking your students? Is there an upcoming bond referendum around the corner? Or do you just want to change the overall perceptions of the schools in the community? Or is there another reason underlying your motivation? It is very important to understand where you want to go, and this will help you determine when you get there.

Analyze your situation. As asked above, are others taking students away from your schools? Is the perception your school is a "tax-wasting parasite" where nothing good happens? This can be done with some of the research mentioned in Chapter Two, but changing an established reputation of public schools should heavily involve teachers. Like the bank teller described in later parts of this chapter, teachers are the front line of relations with your parents and your community. Additionally, there are many more teachers in your community than administrators, and for most people they are the only constant contact they have with schools. They are vital, important, and are often the key to your success.

Analysis is key to develop a marketing orientation. Later on we will talk about planning, implementation, and evaluation.

Implementing Your Marketing Efforts

An organization's overall marketing strategy guides the annual marketing planning process. Successful implementation of the plan requires the consensus and coordination of all of the organization's functional areas (Lehmann & Winer, 1991). For example, if the goal for a bank is to differentiate itself based on superior customer service, the marketing manager must recognize that the branch employees provide the service. In order for the bank to deliver on that service promise and secure that competitive position, the marketing department will have to research customer's definition of "superior service" and communication—or possibly even train—branch workers how to deliver those key aspects of service. In other words, no amount of advertising can create that superior service brand positioning if what happens inside the bank branch does not match customers' expectations. A comprehensive marketing plan considers all aspects of the marketing mix, attending to every detail in order to ensure the overall marketing strategy is attained.

A marketing plan outlines the activities to be undertaken, along with the timetable and who is responsible for the implementation and how it will be executed. However, as thorough as the plan is, its effectiveness is rooted in three key factors: organizational design, incentives, and communication (Cravens, 1994).

An organization's structure can either foster or hinder the effective implementation of a marketing plan. Large, multi-unit businesses often have intricate marketing organizations, due to the complex nature of the customers being served by the organization. However, an intricate marketing function

"I think it's important to note that we really did try hard."

Cartoonresource/Shutterstock.com

is not a necessity. Organizations with flat, flexible designs can actually encourage communication between units and contribute to the successful implementation of the marketing plan.

Allocating responsibility to the individuals or units whose job it is to implement a particular aspect of the marketing plan is a challenge for many organizations. For this reason, rewards or incentives are another component of successful marketing plan implementation. We recognize the fact that public schools do not have the ability to offer employee bonuses; however, contests or basic employee recognition can go a long way toward providing the motivation necessary to gain the level of employee buy-in needed to ensure the successful implementation of the marketing plan.

Finally, communication—both horizontal and vertical—is vital to any marketing organization. In corporations, the marketing function often serves a pivotal role in collecting and disseminating information related to the implementation of the marketing plan. Methods of communication can include status reports, meetings, or informal communication designed to track how well the plan is being implemented, competitors' actions, or any other internal or external changes in the operating environment that may affect the marketing plan.

Internal and external factors can also affect the success or failure of the marketing plan's implementation (Cravens, 1994). Internally, an organization that has adopted a marketing orientation will have the greatest chance at successfully implementing the marketing plan. Put simply, this means that every function in the organization (including finance and operations) has adopted a customer-centric focus. External consultants or suppliers can also affect the marketing plan's success. These can include advertising or PR firms, printing companies, or any other outside businesses that support the marketing plan. Because these external functions do not play a direct role in serving the organization's customers, it is important that their responsibilities are clearly defined and communicated.

As we have outlined, the successful implementation of a marketing plan is as much a function of the ideas contained in the plan, as the coordination and management of the activities that support the plan—and the individuals or groups responsible for their execution.

Get everybody onboard: bus drivers, coaches, secretaries, other administrators, and especially the teachers. People form their opinions of organizations based on the personal interactions with just a few employees. Most people have no understanding of the reach and complexity of a public school, but they know the bus driver who picks up their kids, or the teacher who also coaches soccer and plays "favorites" and sometimes seems rude. Or the time they came to pick up their kid from school and all the signs outside the school say visitors must report to the office, but within the school was confusion, seemed obtuse, and there were no signs pointing toward the office and no one to help.

All public school employees need to understand they are representatives of the school at <u>all</u> times, not just at open houses and established meet-and-greets. Teachers have always been under heightened scrutiny in the US and this has meant having high standards for employees. Below is an example from about 100 years ago. Clearly, there have been high expectations for school employees' behavior. Truly, the lifestyle of a schoolteacher has changed radically in the last 50 or 60 years. For example, a 1915 teachers' magazine listed the following rules of conduct for teachers of that day.

RULES FOR 1915 SCHOOLTEACHERS

- ► You will not marry during the term of your contract.
- ► You are not to keep company with men.
- ► You must be home between the hours of 8 pm and 6 am unless attending a school function.
- ► You may not loiter downtown in any of the ice cream stores.
- ► You may not travel beyond the city limits unless you have the permission of the chairman of the board.

- ► You may not ride in a carriage or automobile with any man unless he is your father or brother.
- ► You may not smoke cigarettes.
- ► You may under no circumstances dye your hair.
- ► You may not dress in bright colors.
- ► You must wear at least two petticoats.
- ► Your dresses must not be any shorter than two inches above your ankle.
- ► To keep the schoolroom neat and clean, you must: scrub the floor at least once a week with hot, soapy water; clean the blackboards at least once a day; and start the fire at 7 am so the room will be warm by 8 am.

(Pennsylvania State Education Association, 2013).[end EXT]

In the next section, we will address methods for evaluating the marketing plan.

Evaluating the Impact of Your Plan

The age-old management expression that a "mediocre strategy well executed is better than a great strategy poorly executed" (Martin, 2010) highlights the importance of measuring the marketing plan. Strategic evaluation helps ensure that performance matches objectives. There are three types of evaluation (Cravens, 1994). The first seeks to identify new opportunities or threats. The second form of evaluation looks to keep marketing performance in line with management expectations. The third form of evaluation is used to solve problems.

iQoncept/Shutterstock.com

The marketing plan is established to achieve specific performance objectives, such as revenue, consumer awareness, or market share. Progress toward the objectives should be measured on a continuing basis. Sales-oriented organizations, for example, focus regularly on four key measures of effectiveness: sales volume, sales growth, profitability, and customer satisfaction (Cravens, Ingram, LaForge, & Young, 1992). Organizations should identify the manner in which they will collect data to be used for performance measures—either through internal sources, through other industry or subscription-based research services, or by conducting their own annual measurements, such as customer surveys.

In some cases, organizations conduct a full-blown audit of their marketing activities. The marketing audit considers not only the internal or external variables that impact the marketing plan, but reviews the plan itself. The purpose is to identify gaps or deficiencies that are not being addressed by the current marketing plan or by the organization's existing marketing framework (Goetsch, 1983). The marketing audit goes beyond standard performance measures and looks at the organization's culture, in terms of its commitment to a marketing orientation and the internal systems that support the marketing effort. It also extensively examines the products and services offered by the organization, the existing market conditions and customer profile, the competitive environment and the promotional activities that support product sales.

Whether or not an organization undertakes a marketing audit, the methods, timetable, and responsibilities for measurement should be identified by the organization, prior to the implementation of the marketing plan. However, beyond collecting the information, the organization must evaluate the data and use it to take corrective action—either to correct weaknesses or maintain strengths. Often referred to as Annual Plan Control (Kotler & Keller, 2012), the evaluation process needs to be consistent and objective, occur at regular intervals appropriate to the activities contained in the marketing plan, and apply to all levels of the organization.

The Marketing Process for Public Schools

The strategic planning process is not a new concept for public schools; however, the introduction of strategic marketing planning is likely quite novel. As we will discuss throughout the book, public schools, for the most part, have enjoyed a steadily supplied customer base for the services they provide. Recent changes to the educational landscape, including charter schools, vouchers, and even on-line educational options, have transformed the competitive environment for education—resulting in the need for schools to more actively market themselves. Nonetheless, while there are specific case-study examples where public schools have been able to successfully market to their audience, the marketing planning and implementation process is not traditionally thought of as a public school administrator's responsibility.

Although marketing is not customarily associated with public schools, the process is not at all unknown to private schools. Private schools have long recognized the need for a well-organized and efficient marketing operation. In order to give public school educators an idea of the kind of marketing activities that their private school counterparts engage in, we have interviewed several private school heads and marketing directors about their strategic marketing operation. In this section, we will review the steps in the marketing planning process by highlighting some of the tips and suggestions offered by private P–12 school administrators, along with private high school marketers.

Beginning with target market identification, most private schools identify anywhere from three to six separate target audiences. These include students (and potential students), parents (and potential parents), alums, faculty, board members, and the community at-large. The structure of the marketing team is often designed to support these target audiences. Positions include a communications or marketing director, along with an admissions staff, and alumni relations and/or development staff. In most cases, the marketing/communications team also includes the head of school, individuals who actively participate in the marketing planning process, as well as contribute to and review the messages that are a part of the communications process.

The planning process for private schools takes several different forms. Most private schools have a long-range, five- or ten-year plan, addressing the long-term vision for the growth and development of the school. The marketing function is an important component of the long-range plan. However, these schools also develop annual marketing plans that will help them achieve their specific performance goals in admissions or development, for example. In one Midwestern P–12 school, the planning process begins over the summer. Here, major marketing goals and communication themes are mapped out for the coming year. In addition, the methods by which these themes will be communicated are also reviewed, in much the same way that a magazine outlines an annual editorial agenda. Most private schools have a number of different communications vehicles, ranging from quarterly or semiannual printed magazines that are mailed out to every stakeholder group, to monthly or weekly online blogs or newsletters directed to parents, faculty, and board members, to weekly letters from school division heads (early childhood, elementary school, middle school, and high school) e-mailed to families. In fact, one school communications director noted that the shift to electronic forms of communication has not only allowed the school to reduce its marketing costs for printing but increase its timeliness and turn-around.

While there are many marketing objectives outlined by private schools, the foremost objective is admissions. With that in mind, the marketing activities are structured to support the admissions cycle. Open houses, tours, parent breakfasts or coffees, student shadow dates, and admissions test dates are among the event-focused activities designed to attract families to schools. As one Midwestern college preparatory high school noted, the goal is to get people in the building so they can experience the culture and visualize the experience. Time spent on campus is especially important for prospective middle and high school students. These schools understand that a significant portion of a student's waking day is spent at school. For early childhood and elementary schools, both the parents and the child must be comfortable in the environment. Private schools appreciate that a school decision is emotional as much as it is logical.

Well-designed collateral materials and websites further support the school's marketing effort. Beyond the communications magazines and newsletters, schools have admissions and fund-raising materials reinforcing the positioning of the school. Private schools understand their operating environment extremely well and do an effective job of differentiating themselves from their competitors. Mission statements and philosophies are clearly communicated in positioning slogans, learning pillars, hallmarks, or core values. Below are examples of how private schools use these themes to readily communicate their distinguishing characteristics.

Sample Positioning Slogans

Knowledge and Values for a Lifetime
Celebrating 200 Years
Experience the Difference
Engaged in Learning. Engaged in Life.

Sample Core Values/Hallmarks/Pillars

Small by design. Rigorous. Relevant. Participatory. Students are known. Faith. Classic Curriculum. Civic Responsibility. Service. Global Readiness. Leadership. Caring. Excellence. Responsibility. Integrity. Respect. Personal Discipline. Compassion. Engaged. Global. United. Impactful. Differentiated. Supportive. Constructive. Connected. Successful. Critical Thinking. Ethical Judgment and Action. Global Citizenship and Cultural Competence. Relational. Developmental. Innovative. Constructivist. Involved. Transformative. Traditional. Inviting. Inclusive. Respectful. Challenging. Visionary.

As can be seen, these are more than just advertising headlines. The pillars and hallmarks represent the core product (service) being sold to customers and delivered to students. They are at the heart of the school's value exchange. These schools consistently communicate the differentiating features of their programs in their marketing materials. More importantly, these themes serve as the distinguishing features of the educational product and give prospective families and students a sense of the intangible benefits being offered by the school.

In terms of the budgetary planning to support the marketing program, anywhere from 2–5% of a school's operating budget is devoted to marketing/admissions/alumni relations and development. Chapter Seven will discuss in greater detail some of the specific promotional activities schools implement to help achieve their marketing objectives. However, many schools use specific metrics to identify whether or not their implementation efforts are on pace to meet the performance objective. For example, where admissions are concerned, schools will track traffic patterns, such as attendance at open houses and number of scheduled shadow visits in order to ensure they are on pace to meet their application and admissions goals.

Where private schools excel in the strategic marketing process is with evaluation. Private schools take the time to collect formal and informal feedback from their various constituencies. They use the responses not only to inform future marketing planning but also to identify the perceived strengths and weaknesses of their overall operation, so they can address issues accordingly. Some schools participate in formal, industry-sponsored surveys. For example, the Independent Schools of the Central States (ISACS) offers member schools the opportunity to participate in surveys they conduct. The results not only provide participating schools with valuable feedback on their own performance, but also allow for benchmark comparisons to other private schools. However, many schools collect their own data, using formal quantitative surveys, along with a variety of qualitative methods, such as parent conversations and student focus groups. For example, one school had students in a rhetoric class examine its admission materials. The valuable feedback alerted the marketing team to subtle themes and underlying messages that students keenly perceive. In one instance, students noted that a picture showing a student talking on a cell phone was already outdated—in a brochure that was only two years old. Not only was the phone technology outmoded, but also students today are more likely to text, rather than speak on the phone. The school's communication director noted that adults would be less apt to pick up on that image but recognized the importance of the observation, noting that the school didn't want its image to be viewed as old or dated. As a result, the school makes it a point to minimize photographic depictions of personal technology or other quickly dated fads in its marketing materials. Using both quantitative and qualitative data allows schools to make changes to the marketing mix and better meet the needs of their target customers.

The strategic marketing process allows organizations to effectively plan a marketing program that considers all four of the P's. While many public school districts have public information and communications officers, that role is only one aspect of the marketing function—promotion. We advocate for the adoption of the marketing concept by public schools, one that comprehensively integrates all aspects of product, price, place, and promotion to the value exchange. Recalling Peter Drucker's quote from the start of this chapter:

> Marketing is so basic that it cannot be considered a separate function within the business . . . But it is, first, a central dimension of the entire business.

What separates marketing organizations from all others is the manner in which marketing is viewed. Organizations who do not uphold an integrated marketing concept look upon "marketing" solely as communications. Furthermore, they view that role as an afterthought. For example, they design products and programs first—and then try and figure out where and how to "market" them. Conversely, marketing organizations consider the consumer's needs up front and embrace the strategic marketing planning process as a way to ensure that those needs will be considered through every aspect of the value chain.

Chapter 3—Spotlight: Colonial Grove Strategic Planning Process

Colonial Grove (CG) is a small independent private school offering preschool through high school on one small campus. They prefer to evaluate themselves on what type of individuals they create, rather than a state imposed standard of measurement. They do not strive to be the biggest. They have found their student population "sweet spot" to be between 950–1000. In many ways their goal is not to grow or be the best school for everyone, but they do want to "skim the cream from the top of the milk." They use national metrics and watch other schools around the globe, rather than paying close attention to local politics and competitors. In meetings with school leaders, you hear them talking about education in very family-friendly terms. Ways that people in the community, that may not have a professional background in education, would understand and respond well to. While they are an elite educational experience with countless attributes, they are fabulously approachable and accessible to the untrained eye.

It is not surprising that when it came time for them to become engaged in a new strategic planning process that they broached it in a very transparent and collaborative way. They created a visual representation of their efforts, established a robust steering committee representing various backgrounds and levels of involvement, set an ambitious timeline for a final presentation to their board of directors, and also set three strategic focus areas for their work: Teaching and Learning, Citizenship and Community, and Sustainability and Stewardship. Additionally, they followed a three-phase process to keep their efforts focused and moving forward.

Phase 1: Learning Phase

The first phase consisted of approximately three months of data collection. This involved talking with lots of people in the community, especially people that had no connection to their school. They wanted to know what people outside of the CG experience thought about their school. They specifically sought to find out how they were perceived by others. They also did comprehensive demographic analysis to find out who would be likely to choose them and how far away families would drive to attend their school.

Phase 2: Distillation Phase

The second phase of the strategic planning process included data analysis and member checking. They made sure all of the data they collected was accurate and then began to piece together what they learned in a meaningful way using their visual representation, steering committee, and three focus areas as their guides.

Phase 3: Document Creation Phase

The third phase of the process involved working on action items and creating documentation of their next steps. They created documents and a plan which they presented to the Board of Directors and kicked off in the fall of the next school year.

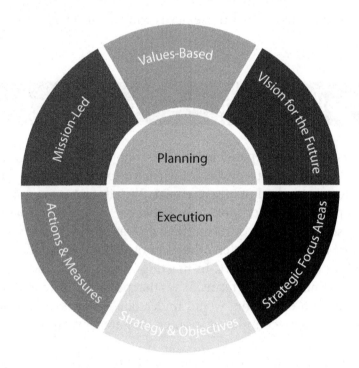

Timeline of Planning Process

Steering Committee Kick-Off Meeting	August 2013
Learning Sessions Conducted	Sept–Oct 2013
Refine and Distill Input/Feedback	End of Oct 2013
Present Draft CG 2020 Strategy to Board	November 2013
Draft Strategy Presented, Discussed, Debated	Q1 2014
Action Items, Milestones, and Measures Developed	Q1 2014
CG 2020 Strategic Plan Finalized/Approved by Board	End of Q1 2014
Planning and Preparation for Kick-Off Event	Q2 2014
Publish and Rollout CG 2020 Strategic Plan	Summer 2014
CG 2020 Kick-Off Event	Fall 2014

Questions

1. In what ways does your school incorporate marketing in their strategic planning process?
2. How does your school differentiate it's strategic planning when: a. planning for new products, b. managing strategies for existing successful products, and c. developing programs for unsuccessful products?
3. Compare your school's strategic planning process with Colonial Grove. How are they the same? How are they different?
4. How does your school's strategic planning process incorporate market research data and situation analysis?

Applying the Concepts

1. Perform an analysis of the market(s) your school currently serves. What are the needs of each market segment? Is your school meeting those needs?
2. Perform a situation analysis of your current operating environment. What are the economic and other business-climate conditions facing your school? Identify problems and opportunities currently being faced.
3. Assess whether or not your organization has a marketing orientation.

References

Armstrong, G., & Kotler, P. (2013). *Marketing: An Introduction* (11th ed.). Boston, MA: Pearson.

Borden, N. (1984). The Concept of the Marketing Mix. *Journal of Advertising Research (Supplement) 24*(4), 7–12.

Cravens, D. (1994). *Strategic Marketing* (4th ed.). Boston, MA: Irwin.

Cravens, D., Ingram, T., LaForge, R., & Young, C. (1992). Hallmarks of effective sales organizations. *Marketing Management*, Winter, 59.

Goetsch, H. (1983). Conduct a comprehensive marketing audit to improve marketing planning. *Marketing News* (March) 14. Retrieved from http://www.marketingpower.com/ResourceLibrary/Publications/ MarketingNews/1983/17/6/19052581.pdf

Kotler, P. (1988). *Marketing Management: Analysis, Planning, Implementation and Control* (6th ed.). Englewood Cliffs, NJ: Prentice Hall.

Kotler, P., & Keller, K. (2012). *Marketing Management* (14th ed.). Boston, MA: Prentice Hall.

Lehmann, D., & Winer, R. (1991). Analysis for Marketing Planning (2nd ed.). Homewood, IL: Richard D. Irwin.

Martin, R. (2010). The execution trap. *Harvard Business Review*. Retrieved from http://hbr.org/2010/07/ the-execution-trap/ar/1\ Chapter 4: Product

Pennsylvania State Education Association. (2013). *Rules for teachers 1915*. Retrieved from http:// oldtowncoldspring.tripod.com/school1.html

Chapter 4

Product

The more alike two products are, the more important their differences become.

—*Regis McKenna, Marketing Guru from Apple, America Online and Microsoft*

The product is the thing of value that is at the heart of the value exchange. It is the good or service for which consumers are willing to exchange something of value in return. In this chapter, we will discuss the manner in which products are developed and managed by organizations, along with the different stages that exist within the life of a product. Within this framework, we will evaluate public school education as a product and discuss the unique operating and competitive characteristics affecting the industry.

Stuart Miles./Shutterstock.com

83

Section One: Distinguishing Products From Services

To begin, we should distinguish that within the Marketing Mix, the term Product is used to represent both products and services. Products are defined as anything offered for use or consumption to satisfy a need or want (Armstrong & Kotler, 2013). Products are physical, tangible goods that can be classified in terms of Consumer products and Industrial products. Consumers products can be classified based on the level of purchasing effort consumers expend in order to attain them (Murphy & Enis, 1986). They include:

▶ Convenience products—items that are frequently purchased and with minimal shopping effort. Examples include soda or bread.

▶ Shopping products—items that are purchased occasionally and for which the consumer is willing to expend some effort to compare options, based on styling, price, or quality. Examples include clothing, shoes, or small appliances.

▶ Specialty products—items that are infrequently purchased and for which consumers make an extensive purchasing effort. Examples include houses, cars, or major appliances.

▶ Unsought products—items the consumer does not normally think about purchasing and require considerable promotion in order to get them to consider for purchase. Examples include pre-paid funerals or life insurance.

For some, the choice of a school is a like a convenience product, made with minimal shopping effort. For others, however, the choice of a school is a specialty product, where the parent(s) give it great thought and effort.

The Industrial products classification groups items that are purchased by organizations for a variety of purposes. These include raw materials and parts, which are used in the manufacturing process. Just a few of the materials used to produce a car, for example, are steel and nuts and bolts. Other

Vaju Ariel/Shutterstock.com

types of industrial products include capital items, which are used for production or operations. This encompasses a wide range of items, such as buildings, machinery, furniture, and office equipment. Finally, supplies and services purchased by an organization to run the business are also included in the industrial products classification. This covers everything from office and janitorial supplies to legal, accounting, advertising, or consulting services.

A service is defined as any act or performance one party can offer to another that is essentially intangible and does not result in the ownership of anything (Kotler & Keller, 2012). Services are the fastest growing component of the world's economy, comprising nearly two thirds of the gross world product (World Economy Profile, 2014). Because of the intangible nature of services, organizations must carefully consider four important characteristics when planning and managing a service business: intangibility, inseparability, variability, and perishability. Intangibility refers to the elusive, untouchable nature of products; as such, they cannot be experienced prior to purchase. Inseparability signifies the service cannot be separated from the service provider. Variability recognizes the quality of the service delivered depends greatly on the experience and expertise of the service provider. As a result, organizations must focus on hiring well-skilled employees and training them to deliver a service that is consistent—not only time after time but also among the various providers. Persishability underscores the fact that, unlike physical products, services cannot be inventoried. As a result, time management becomes an important factor for service businesses. For example, restaurants carefully manage labor expenses based on the flow of business, which is lighter earlier in the week and heavier on the weekend. Restaurants will schedule more wait staff when traffic is greater and be more likely to offer promotional discounts on days when demand is lower. Services are ever mindful of the need to balance these four characteristics in such a way that maximizes productivity but does not undermine the quality of the service experience.

The range of services is also varied (Lovelock, 1996). For example, some are automated, such as coin operated merry-go-rounds or automatic car washes. Others are people-driven, such as accounting or hairstyling. Some services require the customer's presence, such as a haircut, while others do not, such as a courier services. Finally—and perhaps most importantly for education—are the organizational objectives (profit or nonprofit) and ownership (private or public). As a result, the marketing strategies for various service businesses will differ greatly from each other.

In addition, because service quality is variable, it is difficult for consumers to judge them. Further, due to the intangible nature of a service, consumers can only truly evaluate them after the purchase (Ostrom & Iacobucci, 1995). Some services are high in experience qualities, such as amusement parks and haircuts, while others are high in credence qualities, like medical or legal services and automotive repair. Credence quality services are the most difficult for consumers to evaluate after the purchase. For example, a client may determine that he was kindly or respectfully treated by a lawyer and received a reasonable resolution to the matter at hand. However, the client is not necessarily in the position to evaluate whether or not the service provided was the best possible.

Because people typically deliver services, service-oriented businesses focus on maximizing the relationship between both the employee and the consumer. The service profit chain is the term used to describe the link between the employee's effort and the customer's satisfaction (Yee, Yeung, & Cheng, 2011). The links in the service profit chain include:

▶ Internal service quality—superior employee selection and training, a positive work environment, and effective customer-service systems. This results in . . .
▶ Satisfied and productive service employees—satisfied, productive and dedicated employees. This results in . . .
▶ Greater service value—effective and efficient service delivery. This results in . . .
▶ Satisfied and loyal customers—who are loyal, make repeat purchases, and refer other customers. This results in . . .
▶ Healthy service profits and organizational growth—which can be considered characteristics of a superior service firm.

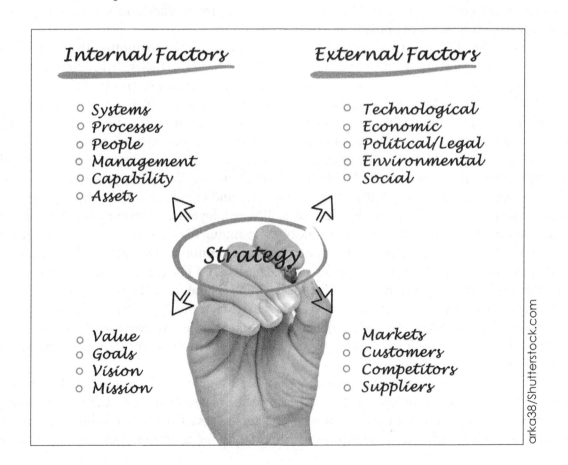

arka38/Shutterstock.com

Recognizing the link between employees and services, excellence in service marketing is a function of external marketing, internal marketing, and interactive marketing (Gronroos, 1984). External marketing describes the activities related to the delivery of the marketing mix activities for customers. Internal marketing defines the training and motivational activities aimed at employees, to encourage superior service. Interactive marketing characterizes the employees' skills in service customers, recognizing that service quality is tested and measured with every interaction a customer has with the employees of the service organization. Former Scandinavian Air System executive Jan Carlzon refers to these encounters as moments of truth— "an episode in which a customer comes into contact with any aspect of the company, however remote, and thereby has an opportunity to form an impression" (Albrecht & Zemke, 1985, p. 27). Public education is filled with these opportunities. That is why public school employees must understand that <u>every</u> interaction forms an opinion of the school.

Service marketing excellence requires organizations to effectively differentiate their offerings. This can be accomplished in a number of ways, but must incorporate the people and processes through which the service is delivered. Services can differentiate themselves on two levels: primary and secondary (Kotler & Keller, 2012). The primary service package relates to customer expectations of the fundamental service to be provided. Here an organization can differentiate itself based on a number of variables, such as quality, timeliness, or price. Service providers can also differentiate themselves by adding secondary service features, which can include any number of ancillary service components that enhance the service value.

In the next section, we will consider the unique characteristics that classify education as a service and review the challenges public schools face in building and maintaining an effective service-oriented organization, without sacrificing the long-standing, expected standards of instruction and learning.

Chatchawan/Shutterstock.com

Education as a Service

As was pointed out in the first part of this chapter, education is clearly a service. The main characteristic of a service is that production and consumption occur simultaneously, and cannot be separated from each other. Education is important because with each student taught, there is expanded knowledge. This is different from a product in that when one transfers the product to another (or sells), the original owner of the product loses either control or possession of the product and its contents. The same is not true in education, where the service provided, educating others, expands the content basis, and there is no loss of the originator's knowledge, and in fact the originators (or teachers) may be expanded by sharing with others. This comes from either improvements (by the teacher) in the ability to understand the concept shared, and from the individuals being taught and their expansion of the knowledge base.

Knowing that education is a service, and not a product, can help with understanding marketing, and also to begin to explain why marketing of education is so very difficult. Tangible items are easier for laypeople to comprehend as products. It is much easier to see a bicycle tire as a product, because it is something one can hold and easily understand its uses. Education is not tangible in that manner, and takes on many forms. Additionally, some people have very positive views of education and their experiences in school, while others have very negative views of the role of education and what it has done to assist them in their development.

Building on the previous section and its discussion of external, internal, and interactive marketing, it is important to appreciate how these three factors influence public education. These chapters lay the groundwork for how public schools should develop a marketing program. Most individuals think of a marketing program solely with external marketing, negating the internal and interactive marketing. All three are vital to understanding the role of marketing and need to be used effectively to help others *value* public education.

External marketing is the delivery of the marketing mix activities for the customers. This is the main purpose of public education, but specifically defining this service for others is very difficult. For some, education is the teaching of basic skills necessary to participate in a democracy; for others, it involves such lofty goals as to teach the love of exploration, or to prepare students to contribute to an ever-evolving society. While for others, the sole purpose of education is to teach reading, writing, and math. Given how difficult it is to define the role of education, and what it means for others, can make external marketing efforts very difficult.

As a service, education is one of the hardest to define but it is important to point out the many different ways in which public schools provide customer satisfaction as one means of external marketing. This also can take on different meanings based on the customers one might have. As has been noted in previous chapters, defining the customer is very important. Specifics for addressing these groups will be addressed in subsequent chapters, however, public schools need to be aware of how they address many different issues as a part of their external marketing mix, and they include: reports about school safety, results from high school student engagement surveys, numbers of students who graduate, numbers of students who go on to higher education, number of students who are deemed proficient in the state assessments. All of these are factors that help others understand the role public education plays in the community. They are not at all definitive, but can help non-educators get a glimpse of what goes on in schools.

Internal marketing is different from external marketing. The focus of internal marketing defines the training and motivational activities aimed at employees, to encourage superior service. This is vital to public education. Public education is a service industry—a hard one to define, but still a service industry. How to provide for and train staff for providing superior educational service is difficult, but necessary. Without employees understanding what is necessary, and then providing it to the students and parents, it would be all but impossible to convince others that public education is not only doing its job, but also doing it well.

How do we train and motivate public school staff to provide superior educational service? Some accomplish this through mission statements, where everyone knows the goals of the organization and hopefully uses this to make decisions about the implementation of services for students. Others do this through bringing in speakers who have skills to motivate public school staff to meet the needs of the ever-changing population of students and parents.

Some of the best ways, however, are through hiring decisions and modeling of behavior. When hiring, make sure the applicant not only has the credentials for the position they are seeking, but spend a serious amount of time considering whether the school district would like this individual to be the face and contact for everyone. As a public school employee, either as a teacher or as a staff member, they will be held to a different standard in the public and for many people will be a main point of contact for others in the district, representing everything the district is trying to accomplish. For parents, their child's teacher is the face of the district. For others in the community, this person will be identified as a teacher, representing all education. Take this consideration seriously, because if the person can be effective in dealing with others and representing the school district well, they can convince others of the strength of what is happening that they will never see.

The next best thing to do to help with internal marketing is modeling. The leaders of the school need to model the behavior (or behaviors) they expect others to emulate. This can include what is said in front of parents and others and what is said when parents are not around. Yes, these are two different things, but how public schools deal with students, parents, and others who are using the educational service, and how they are treated can lead to <u>others</u> emulating and learning what needs to be done to be successful in their interactions with <u>others</u>. Make sure the school leaders model for all to see what happens when a parent comes in with a complaint. Much of the time the parent only wants to be heard and treated with respect, not necessarily expecting to get everything they want. The important part is how schools deal with parents when they are upset. The emotions and the memories from these experiences will be around for a long time and potentially shared with many others.

Have the school leaders model respect and listening, and make sure those who need to be involved are, and understand the importance of the situation. Also, after a parents who has been complaining about the school (no matter how small or trivial the complaint may be), make sure to address the complaint, work to make sure corrective actions are in place, and not to talk negatively about the "crazy" parent. It is very easy to dismiss <u>the parent</u> and call <u>them</u> names, however, this sets a tone for others and is easily emulated. Prevent it from happening by modeling that all parents' complaints and comments need to be taken seriously.

The last form of marketing public schools needs to focus on is that of interactive marketing. Interactive marketing characterizes the employees' skill in service customers, recognizing that service quality is tested and measured with every interaction a customer has with the employees of the organization. For public schools this takes on many, many forms. As noted in other sections of this chapter, every contact with a student, every contact with a parent, every contact with a person in the community is an opportunity to represent the face of the public schools.

The impact of a good interaction can be dramatic and have a lifelong influence on someone. Most people, even many years removed from public education, can remember something either a teacher or staff member did to help them get through a lesson or just a bad day. This is impossible to quantify. As a service organization, this is what public education does. It lays the groundwork for others to benefit in the future from what they are doing today. The lessons learned in a kindergarten classroom will likely be lessons used many years down the road, but help with the citizenship aspects expected of public schools. The famous book by Robert Fulghum (Fulghum, 1989) summarized some of the main things learned in kindergarten: share everything, play fair, put things back where you found them, don't take things that aren't yours, live a balanced life, are some of the things taught in kindergarten. The service provided to the kindergarteners and their parents is lifelong and can help these children be effective members of our society. The same thing can be said of the reading and math instruction in second and third grade. It is lifelong, beneficial, and a great service to the children and their parents.

For a consumer to understand education, and because of the lack of tangibility of what it provides, there needs to be an understanding of the value of the services, which for some can be very different to understand. The value of education as a service is hard to explain. When a company develops a product, the product has a defined use. There may be other products the company develops that have similar uses and many provide more uses or more refined uses, but all are clearly defined. The service provided by public education is harder to define. In fact, education as a service may be impossible to define because of the many roles education takes with all the varied interests of the students and families involved with the programs. Education as a service for students with severe intellectual disabilities is going to be very different from the educational service for students in the junior year of high school that are seeking to go to an Ivy League college after high school.

There are also many factors influencing education, with one of the biggest recently being No Child Left Behind (NCLB). One element integral to NCLB is a report on the district's "Adequate Yearly Progress" (AYP), or an annual record of how well each school helps the local district obtain agreed-upon goals to ensure student achievement and school accountability. AYP focuses on increasing the academic performance of all public school students, and on improving the performance of low-performing schools. Additionally, AYP, as an NCLB mandate, underscores proficiency expectations in reading achievement, mathematics achievement, attendance, participation on state assessment, and graduation rates by 2014.

To obtain data necessary to report local and state AYP, each public school and district within the state must collect performance data on individual students and individual schools within districts. Building principals help their stakeholders to locate and identify each student and group of students within the district, measuring achievement progress on an annual basis. Additionally, parents and guardians receive individual achievement data about where their child stands academically on statewide assessment and/or alternative assessment procedures, and whether their local schools and districts are succeeding in meeting state standards. Such AYP standards are meant to hold schools accountable for the achievement of all students. For a majority of students, AYP standards rely on students' scores on "high-stakes standardized tests" in the form of statewide assessment. High-stakes standardized tests can be best defined as tests that contain unvarying inquiry and scoring used to make major decisions about students, including grade retention and graduation rates.

There are other factors making demands on public education, and the landscape will be continually changing. Soon, public education will be implementing the Common Core Curriculum, all the while being held accountable for annual yearly progress under NCLB or ESEA. As a service, many of these requirements make it difficult to focus on all the demands being placed on public education, but it is the qualitative differences that become important.

Because education as a service is hard to define, it makes it very difficult to understand qualitative differences. The effectiveness of a bike tire and whether it does its job is a quick and easy measurement. It either fits on the bicycle and rolls down the road on the rim as expected or not. Services are much harder to determine whether they are quality or not. Many have attempted to place a value on education, looking at a variety of factors including long-term earnings, incarceration rates, and post high school graduate education status, including socio economic status. These are all ways to help "sell" others on the imperative for becoming educated, but they do not represent the complete picture of the importance and need of education. There are many former public school students who have severe disabilities who are much more independent due to the educational service provided to them while they were involved in K–12 education. There are also individuals who have received a lot of higher education and do not have a high income because of choices they have made about where to live and how much they want to work. Finally, there are many examples of individuals who many years after leaving school, remember a fact or saying a teacher said to them that helps them for that one instant and provides what is needed to solve the problem. As a service, these facts are in large part why the service of education is so difficult to describe.

Finally, as a service, one of the biggest differences is the ability to return a product when it does not work or is ineffective. A defective bike tire is a tangible product that can be returned to the point of purchase for the possibility of an exchange or refund. When a service such as education is not effective, or does not do its job, one does not have the ability to return the product. Also, it may take a long time to determine that education was not effective.

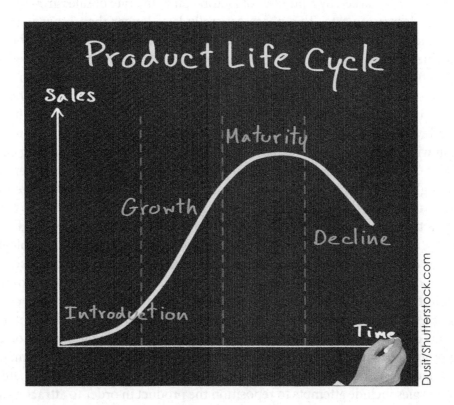

Dusit/Shutterstock.com

The Product Life Cycle

As we have reviewed, most organizations operate in a competitive environment. With that in mind, there are any number of competitive dynamics that affect the marketing mix strategy employed. While the goal of every organization is to enjoy continued growth over time, many business organizations recognize that products and services have a natural cycle. The product life cycle concept is based on the fact that "a product's sales volume follows a typical four-phase cycle" (Clifford, 1965, p. 34). The stages in the product life cycle include introduction, growth, maturity, and decline. In this section, we will review each phase and discuss the market conditions that exist, along with the strategies organizations can employ to remain competitive.

In the introduction stage, the product concept is new and enters the marketplace. During this period, sales are slow and profits are negative, due to the tremendous costs the organization must incur to produce, distribute, and promote the product. Heavy promotion is necessary to educate consumers about the product in terms of what it is, why they need it, where to get it, and what they should expect to pay for it. There are few, if any, competitors in this phase, as the product concept is new and untested. As a result, only basic versions of the product concept are available.

Once the product gains a foothold in the market and becomes accepted, it enters the growth stage. During this stage, sales increase at an increasing rate. Recognizing the sales opportunity existing within the product category, other competitors will enter the market as well. They will most likely introduce other variations on the product, which, in turn, will attract new customers to the market. In return, the organization will focus its own marketing strategy on product improvements. The promotional strategy will shift from awareness building to reinforcing the product's positioning to differentiate itself from the growing number of competitors.

The maturity stage is marked by a number of factors. First, the rate of sales growth slows, meaning sales increase at a decreasing rate. This phase generally lasts longer than other periods. The slow-down in sales is the result of the fact that product concept is widely accepted and there are few new customers available to expand demand. In addition, there are no new competitors entering the market, so market share is fixed. As a result, sales growth to new customers is more difficult to realize. However, organizations will try to modify aspects of the marketing mix to expand the market and increase sales. This can be done in a number of ways. For example, the organization may try to find new market segments for its brands or it may alter the product in order to attract new users. In terms of price, the organization will lower price as a means of increasing market share by attracting customers from other competitors. As a result of the increased competition, weaker competitors either drop out of the market or are bought out by larger or more stable companies. Promotional strategies employed in this phase are those that support the revised product or pricing strategies.

In the decline stage, sales decrease and continue to do so at an increasing rate. The decline phase can occur for a number of reasons. For example, other product introductions or technological advances may usurp the product's usefulness, just as records were outmoded by compact discs. Demand can also decrease due to any number of demographic or cultural factors that result in an overall decreased number of customers who desire to purchase the product, as has been the case with cigarettes. Faced with declining sales, the organization has a limited number of options. In order to maintain profits, organizations can cut costs. This could include cutting labor or reducing the size or quality of the product being produced, without changing the price. Organizations must carefully manage products in the decline stage and determine whether or not they should maintain or eliminate the product. Maintenance strategies include attempts to reposition the product in order to attract customers to use the product for other purposes. An example of this was when the makers of baking soda—faced with declining sales related to shifts in cooking and baking behavior—repositioned the product based on its deodorizing properties. A decision to drop a product would be to cease production completely or to find a buyer for the product, which was seen with the Hostess Bakery Twinkies brand, which was purchased in 2013 by a private equity firm who recognized the brand's potential (Sanburn, 2013).

It should be noted that not all products proceed through the life cycle at the same pace (Cox, 1967). Some products experience a wave of growth, followed by a leveling off. However, a promotional push is often enough to spur a second wave of sales. The fashion industry provides good examples of products that have life cycles of varying lengths. Fashion fads, for example, enter the market, grow quickly, reach a peak, and then fade out completely. Conversely, fashion classics remain popular for a long time.

Beyond focusing specifically on the life cycle of a particular product category, marketers must also monitor overall market conditions to determine the effects the economy has on sales. In an economic downturn or recession, there are five guidelines a firm can utilize to help direct its decisions.

First, an organization can increase its investment. Research suggests that during a recession, most service-oriented firms under-spend on research and development, and over-spend on advertising, producing a negative effect on profits (Srinivasan, Lilien, & Sridhar, 2011). As a result, these firms are encouraged to increase their spending on research and development and decrease their advertising expenditures in order to improve profits. For publicly held companies, the converse is true: these service firms achieve positive returns in response to increased research and development and promotional spending.

The second option available to firms operating in challenging economic conditions is to get closer to customers (Lay, Hewlin, & Moore, 2009). Because consumers may alter their consumption patterns in response to economic uncertainties, marketers should use this as an opportunity to reach out to customers and find out exactly what they need, and consider adjusting production levels or other aspects of the marketing mix in response in order to remain profitable.

The third option is to review budget allocations (Kotler & Keller, 2012). A recession presents the firm with the opportunity to review spending to determine which marketing-related expenses are producing the greatest return. Out of necessity, many firms discover that newer and cheaper forms of communication resulted in improved sales.

The fourth guideline for organizations is to focus on the most compelling value proposition (Williamson & Zeng, 2009). In short, marketing messages should emphasize the value proposition of a brand, in terms of its financial, logistical, and psychological benefits.

Finally, marketers should evaluate their brand and product offerings (Kotler & Keller, 2012). Firms that produce a portfolio of brands aimed at different markets should place greater emphasis on

Lightspring/Shutterstock.com

brands that target the lower end of the socioeconomic spectrum. In tough economic times, customer spending on most products tends to go down a grade. For example, consumers who may normally purchase items in the mid-range will shift their consumption to the lower-priced options.

Having an understanding of where a product or service stands, not only relative to the competition, but in terms of its life cycle stage helps marketers develop more effective marketing strategies. In the next section, we will discuss the life cycle for public education and how increased competition has affected the industry.

The Product Life Cycle for Education

As we stated early in the text, our intentions are not to advocate for or against competition in education. Nor can we, in the scope of this book, cover the full impact of competition on the field. We are, however, discussing how public schools should begin to navigate the new competitive waters within which they find themselves and incorporate effective marketing strategies into their current practice. Educators should begin by utilizing the four characteristics of planning and managing a service business.

From an educator's perspective the four characteristics (Intangibility, Inseparability, Variability, and Perishability) of planning and managing a service business could be interpreted as follows:

Intangibility: Educational experience of students attending your school. Our public schools have a long history of providing high quality education for the masses. The large majority of the populace develops a perspective on schools based on publicized test scores. In most cases families and students believe their educational experience in their public school is good, but believe that all other public schools are bad. Very few families and community members take the time to visit schools their children do not attend. It is very important for public schools to provide the appropriate variety of information to the community, so that the community as a whole, without ever walking in a school building, has a notion of what the educational experience in the building is like.

Inseparability: What is that thing that differentiates you from your competitors? What is it that families and students can only get from your school? For some students and families this may be the perceived prestige that comes with being an alumnus of your institution. For others it may be the availability of an original program. In some cases students and families want to be part of your institutional traditions and want to feel like part of your school community.

Variability: Our schools are only as good as the school staff. This seems like a no-brainer, but the field of education has spent considerable time in recent years trying to quantify the impact of teachers and administrators on student achievement. Not surprisingly, most researchers agree that highly qualified teachers and administrators illicit higher test scores and provide a superior educational experience for students.

Perishability: Empty schools are lost income. In most state funding formulas the end result is that each student represents state and federal dollars. If you have classrooms that are not filled or completely empty, you are losing income. Empty rooms or buildings must still be maintained, heated, and cooled. They need electricity and water, even if they are used very little. Additionally, someone will need to manage and maintain these buildings, and in some cases provide security. Once your final student counts are in to the state, any empty seat is lost income for that year which can never be recovered. Every student lost to a competitor is lost income for your school that you can never get back.

In addition to the four characteristics of planning and managing a service business, administrators should also consider the links in their profit chain. To work proactively as a service business, schools must examine the links in their service profit chain (Yee, Yeung, & Cheng, 2011). For schools, aligned service chain links are as follows:

- Internal Service Quality—Hiring highly qualified staff, teachers, and administrators, providing timely and research based professional development, and effective family engagement processes. This results in . . .
- Satisfied and Productive Service Employees—Satisfied, productive, and dedicated staff, teachers, and administrators. This results in . . .
- Greater Service Value—Effective and efficient classrooms, extracurricular activities, interactions with families. This results in . . .
- Satisfied and Loyal Customers—Communities where families and community members are loyal to the school, support the schools in times of need, attend school events, recommend the school to others, and send all of their children to the school. This results in . . .
- Healthy Service Profits and Organizational Growth—Highly functioning schools that have healthy student achievement, popular extracurricular activities, satisfied staff, teachers, and administrators, involved alumni, as well as engaged families and communities.

Unlike many businesses, public schools have a unique situation to navigate. Public schools must adhere to both state and federal mandates that in many cases are not fully funded. In many ways, public school's hands are tied when it comes to cutting costs and can only use monetary funds for designated projects. This means that while a school may have a $10 million budget, they cannot make arbitrary decisions about how to spend or save those dollars. In other business models, administrators have full authority to utilize resources as they deem most beneficial for the health of the organization.

Public education is currently in the third stage of the product life cycle. The third stage is maturity. Public education is facing the following realities:

- Sales Growth Slows: The number of students that are choosing public education is decreasing at an increasing rate. The number of students that are choosing a nonpublic education are increasing.
- Product Concept is Widely Accepted: Public education, in many ways, has been around since the post-industrial era with very few changes. A large majority of the population is familiar with and/or has utilized public education.
- No New Competitors Entering the Market: In natural market conditions the market share is fixed. Given new legislation and policy (vouchers and charters) traditional public education is not facing a natural market in maturity.
- ·Sales Growth to New Customers is Difficult: Public schools are struggling to keep current students and recruit students away from private education.

The importance of the third point cannot be overstated. The impact of unnatural market factors (new competitors) during a fixed time is crucial. The market for public education is shrinking based on population growth, but we are adding more schools. This only increases the stakes for public schools and is pushing toward a declining market. In times like this, public schools must focus on the five guidelines that direct decision-making during a recession:

- Increase Investments
- Get Closer to Customers

- ▶ Review Budget Allocations
- ▶ Focus on the Most Compelling Value Proposition
- ▶ Evaluate Your Brand and Product Offerings

Public education is facing somewhat of a perfect storm. Due to state and federal budget cuts, schools are being forced to provide high-quality services with dwindling budgets. In light of accountability efforts and new legislation, public schools are being forced to put an overemphasis on raising test scores and support students with remedial services in order to meet these new achievement standards. At the same time, families and communities are being offered numerous educational options and are choosing schools based on extracurricular activities. As public schools try to do more with less, many have chosen to put what funding they have into remediation programs to increase test scores to keep state accreditation, but have dropped extracurricular funding in order to make this happen. Unfortunately, this could mean that students and families, who make choices based on extracurricular activities, will not choose these schools, hence their numbers and budget will decrease even more.

Chapter Four—Spotlight: Lynhurst 7th and 8th Grade Center

In 2014 Dan Wilson was named Indiana Middle School principal of the year. He is the presiding principal of Lynhurst 7th & 8th Grade Center (LHC), an urban middle school serving over 1,200 students as part of the Metropolitan School District of Wayne Township, located on the Westside of Indianapolis, IN. LHC is a Title One school where more than 86% of the students receive free & reduced lunch services, 14% of the students have an IEP, and another 14% qualify for English as a new language services. The school is racially diverse with 47% of the students being European, 26% Latino, 20% African American, and 6% identifying as multiracial. Roughly 13% of the student body is comprised of students that are undocumented and LHC has a 30% mobility rate. Over the last 8 years, Dan has worked tirelessly to continue the growth started by his predecessor in turning the school around.

One of Dan's favorite LHC data points is their 100% attendance rate at student led parent teacher conferences. According to Dan, this goal of 100% attendance was a way for him to continue the climate change that was beginning to happen when he took over. "I wanted teachers to know that we could target something meaningful and not just get it done, but knock it out of the park." Dan draws from a Japanese business model that focuses on long-term growth, supports teams as a way to breed loyalty, celebrates employees finding problems and fixing them, all the while recognizing that business is war.

As a staff, LHC decided to implement an aggressive and progressive collaboration style with the families they serve. "Our school serves a community that fights for survival everyday in lots of ways. We want them to know that we are in that fight with them. We will fight for their kids. The only way we can really prove that is to get them in the door." To accomplish this end Dan implemented the following plan:

1. Put teachers in charge. Every year a new set of teachers are put in charge of running student led conferences. He relies heavily on teachers who are going through principal preparation programs.
2. Provide high quality translators. Ensuring that every family and teacher feels comfortable with the conversation is crucial to a successful conference experience.

3. Provide transportation. For many years LHC didn't hit 100% because families couldn't get to school, now we provide a school bus that will pick them up and take them home.
4. Utilize technology. With a few families LHC relies on Skype or home visits in the event that a family member is unable to travel.
5. Provide childcare. LHC partners with a local university to provide childcare for families that have more than one child so they can focus on the conversation with the teacher.
6. Pick a good time. LHC always makes sure that student led conferences are held on multiple evenings and no other school events are allowed to be scheduled.

Questions

1. In what ways is LHC letting families know what they get in exchange for their tax dollars?
2. How has LHC utilized information about its target audience to implement climate change?
3. How does LHC's "aggressive and progressive collaborative" style help them find out what others think of their school?

Applying the Concepts

1. How does your school utilize the four characteristics of Intangibility, Inseparability, Variability, and Perishability?
2. Where do you believe public education is in the product life cycle? Why? What does this mean for your building or district?
3. Is your current educational market saturated? Are the market conditions natural? What does this mean for your overall marketing efforts?

References

Albrecht, K., & Zemke, R. (1985). *Service America. Doing Business in the New Economy.* Homewood, IL: Dow Jones-Irwin.

Armstrong, G., & Kotler, P. (2013). *Marketing: An Introduction* (11th ed.). Boston, MA: Pearson.

Clifford, Jr. D. (1965). Managing the product life cycle. *Management Review, 54*(6), 34–38.

Cox, W. (1967). Product life cycles as marketing models. *Journal of Business, 40*(4), 375–384.

Fulghum, R. (1989). *All I really need to know I learned in kindergarten.* New York: Villard Books.

Gronroos, C. (1984). A service-quality model and its marketing implications. *European Journal of Marketing, 18*(4), 36–44.

Kotler, P., & Keller, K. (2012). *Marketing Management* (14th ed.). Boston, MA: Prentice Hall.

Lay, P., Hewlin, T., & Moore, G. (2009). In a downturn, provoke your customers. *Harvard Business Review 87*(3), 48–56.

Lovelock, C. (1996). S*ervices Marketing, 3rd ed.* Upper Saddle River, NJ: Prentice Hall.

Murphy, P., & Enis, B. (1986). Classifying products strategically. *Journal of Marketing 50* (July) 24–42.

Ostrom, A., & Iacobucci, D. (1995). Consumer trade-offs and the evaluation of services. *Journal of Marketing 59,* 17–28.

Sanburn, J. (2013). How do you revive Twinkies? A Q&A with the new owners: The Metropoulos Brothers. *Time.* Retrieved from http://business.time.com/2013/03/21/how-do-you-revive-twinkies-a-qa-with-the-new-owners-the-metropoulous-brothers/

Srinivasan, R., Lilien, G., & Sridhar, S. (2011). Should firms spend more on research and development and advertising during recessions? *Journal of Marketing, 75*(3), 49–65.

Williamson, P., & Zeng, M. (2009). Value-for-money strategies for recessionary times. *Harvard Business Review, 87*(3), 66–74.

World Economy Profile 2014. http://www.indexmundi.com/world/economy_profile.html

Yee, R., Yeung, A., & Cheng, T. (2011). The service-profit chain: An empirical analysis in high-contact service industries. *International Journal of Production Economics, 130*(2), 236–245.

Chapter 5

Place

Make your product easier to buy than your competition,
or you will find customers buying from them not you.

—Mark Cuban, Co-founder HDNET, Owner of Dallas Mavericks, Landmark Theaters and Magnolia Pictures

A s any good realtor knows, where a business is located is extremely important. Location, location, location. This is typically a strength of public schools. Traditional businesses plan a product placement strategy that will help them deliver products to their customers faster and more efficiently. With this in mind, we introduce another member of the value chain: the marketing intermediary. This can include wholesalers, distributors, and retailers, all of whom help Sellers broaden their distribution capabilities. As we will demonstrate, the middleman—whose name is often spoken with disdain—actually provides efficiencies. In reality, consumers do not go from one manufacturer to purchase shoes, and then to another to buy pants, and so forth. Rather, manufacturers utilize sophisticated logistical systems to send their products through the value chain to retailers who are more conveniently located near the consumer, and who sell other items the consumer may also need or want.

Simply put, marketing channels "can be viewed as sets of interdependent organizations involved in the process of making a product or service available for use or consumption" (Stern & El-Ansary, 1982, p. 3). These include indirect and direct options. Indirect options utilize marketing intermediaries with multiple channels, such as wholesalers and retailers. Others utilize a single channel, sending the product directly from the manufacturer to the retailer, who then sells it to the end user. The direct marketing option is also referred to as a zero channel, where the product is delivered directly from the Seller to the Buyer. Many products are distributed through direct marketing methods, which utilize a variety of promotional means, including catalogs and websites. Education, either in its traditional in-school or online format, is delivered via direct channels. In this chapter, we will discuss the channels of distribution for education.

The Landscape of Education in the US

The sheer number of recent changes in education on both the local and national levels is overwhelming, even for the most savvy and seasoned educator. In many ways, most educators are figuring out how to respond in the moment with little support, guidance, or historical precedence to draw from. There is literally no aspect of education that has not felt some of the recent changes. Chapter Two outlined the specific demographic information on school shoppers. Millions of families across the country have started utilizing their educational options. As public educators move forward, they must consider the value chain of education to gain a full understanding of the current field and chart a path for their public school.

The value chain for public education is the string of groups that work together to provide our society with an educated populace. For public schools the value chain is quite simple given that it delivers a product via a direct channel. The educational value chain starts with families and communities sending their children to the public schools. Then public schools provide students with an education and send them to college or some type of post-secondary educational setting. Educational institutions produce alumni who will be taxpayers and voters, and then become the families and communities that send their children to public schools and the chain starts over again.

In many cases, the simplicity of this model has led many public schools to employ someone to handle communications or public relations. Unfortunately, this has proven for many public schools to be too little too late. This big picture perspective on education as a product is important to keep in mind, but is not the only piece of the story. Given that education is a service, it is also important to define an internal value chain through the lens of service to adequately address the needs of public schools.

According to the *Harvard Business Review* (Martin, 2010), top service agencies recognize the direct correlation between employee satisfaction and customer satisfaction. From an internal perspective, the importance of employee satisfaction cannot be overstated. For public schools, this means staff members who work directly with students and families have the greatest opportunity to make an impact on achievement, retention, and recruitment. Public schools have a long history of understanding the important role staff play in student achievement, but in the era of school choice this is not enough. Public schools must be conscious of retention and recruitment. The educational value chain is as follows:

FIGURE 5.1—External Educational Value Chain

FIGURE 5.2—Internal Educational Value Chain

Each link in the ***Educational Value Chain*** is critical to the health of your public school. A high quality experience for staff would include physical work environment, professional development opportunities, supplies and technology for working with students, and recognition programs. All of these things are vital to ensuring your staff is satisfied. With a satisfied staff, public schools are able to more accurately ensure students are receiving a high quality experience. Families and communities are satisfied with public schools when they provide an educational experience meeting their needs. If families and the larger community are satisfied with the public education offered in their community, they will support the school in times of need. This show of support could be by voting yes to approve levees and/or referendums or could come in the form of sending additional students to your school, as well as referring the public school to other families who are school shopping.

Growth of public schools is the result of family and community loyalty. This loyalty is the result of satisfaction with the value of the educational services the public school provides. Educational staff, through their interactions with students, families, and the community, create the value of public education. Staff are directly impacted by support services and policies encouraging them to support students. When students are supported, families and the community gain trust and develop loyalty to the public school. Public schools with loyal families and communities grow and flourish. As public schools map out clear paths for growth, the entities supporting public schools are also trying to respond.

Public schools are not the only entities impacted by the changes in education. There are countless businesses and governmental agencies supplying and supporting public schools. Since the structure of public schools has been stable and consistent for decades, many outside vendors, governmental agencies, and suppliers have also maintained stable and consistent practices to meet the needs of public schools. As the field of education shifts it causes a ripple effect across these outside vendors, agencies, and suppliers.

Many companies over the years have developed very successful business models for serving schools. As the structure of P–12 schools have changed so must their service delivery model and sometimes their products. In some markets charters and vouchers have been introduced. This means that in some cases, public schools that used to be large are now smaller and some schools that used to be small are now bigger. In other instances, regions of the state that used to have one or two schools, now have five or six.

Many governmental agencies assign workers according to size and region. If these entities have not shifted their own internal practices to reflect the changes in their assigned areas, public schools may be getting missed, while others may be receiving too many services. If public schools have evidence of students not getting the services they are entitled to, you must make sure your school connects with these entities. Make sure they know about the changes in your school and request a plan to address your new needs.

While many traditional public schools are struggling financially, many private schools and charters are eligible for grants, vouchers, and other new forms of funding. This shift in fiscal support has caused many vendors to shift their marketing efforts toward the needs of private schools and

FIGURE 5.3—Educational Supply Map

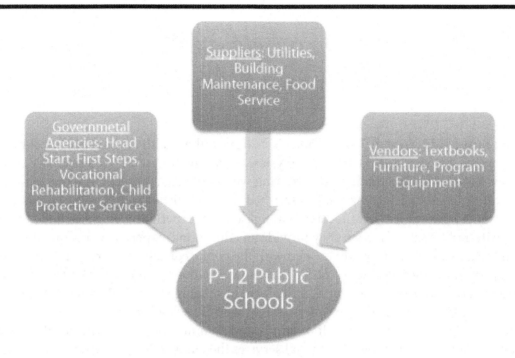

charters. The growth in the markets for suppliers and vendors could ultimately prove to be a good thing for traditional P–12 public schools. Innovation has spurred countless new products focused on education. As the market for educational products expands, many of the suppliers that have historically had larger market shares are also finding themselves in a more competitive market. This results in a public school having a greater ability to bargain with these companies. Additionally, it may be to a public school's fiscal advantage to partner with nearby private or charter schools to share resources and services. To navigate the educational market, it is important to have a basic understanding of each type of school so that you can develop a more holistic picture of your situation. To navigate the educational market, it is important to have a basic understanding of each type of school so that educators can develop a more holistic picture of their situation. The upcoming section shares various types of schools currently found across the US.

Types of Schooling

Students are being served in a variety of different types of schooling. This section provides a description, history, and purpose of the following types of placements for providing education: traditional public schools, charter schools, parochial schools, private schools, and private tutors and homeschooling. Understanding each will help educators tailor the service they provide and allow for a better ability to market public schools. Remember, the purpose of this book is not to complain about or disparage nonpublic schooling. Parochial, private, charter, and homeschooling clearly have a place and is very beneficial to some students. The purpose of this book is to help public school educators to understand the culture of competition they face, and then be able to effectively market based on these facts. Though basic, the following descriptors are here to remind administrators of the place public education has in society and what services to expect from others.

Josef Hanus/Shutterstock.com

Traditional Public Schools

A traditional public school is a school or institution controlled and operated by publicly elected or appointed officials and deriving its primary support from public funds. There is no tuition to attend public schools for residents of the school district. Property taxes pay for most of the cost of public schools. Although public schools get a very small percentage of their funding from donations and parent and student fund-raising efforts, by far the greatest proportion of the money comes from state and local governments. The federal government contributes less than 10% of the cost.

Historically, education was only for children of privilege, but gradually through the nineteenth century it became apparent that a well-educated citizenry and workforce was necessary. States oversee public education, with some guidelines from the federal government. In general, however, local districts oversee the administration of schools, with the exception of licensing requirements and general rules concerning health and safety, which is usually controlled by a state department of education. Since schools rely heavily on local property taxes to meet the vast majority of school expenses, public schools have thus tended to reflect the educational values and financial capabilities of the communities in which they are located.

By the middle of the twentieth century, most states took a more active regulatory role than in the past. The states also became much more responsible for financing education. In 1940 local property taxes financed 68% of public school expenses, while the states contributed 30%. In 1990 local districts and states each contributed 47% to public school revenues.

During the 1980s and 1990s, virtually all states have given unprecedented attention to their role in raising education standards. Most states have implemented reform strategies emphasizing more frequent testing conducted by states, more effective state testing, and more state-mandated curriculum requirements.

The federal government's role in education has increased, especially with the passage of No Child Left Behind in 2001. States and localities are having to implement standards for education with greater attention to federal standards.

Though thought of as public schools, it is important to point out they serve both public and private interests both for businesses to work and for society to have a high enough literacy level to have a functioning democracy. Without a literate citizenry, individuals are less likely to contribute effectively to the well-being of their communities and more likely to be a drain on public resources. Therefore, in a real sense, any school that helps children master reading, writing, mathematics, and other essential content is already advancing some rather significant public purposes.

Public schools have the responsibility for teaching the principles, habits, and obligations of citizenship. Public schools, using public funds, teach children the essential skills and knowledge that make for productive citizens, and instruct them in the framework of rights and obligations of being a citizen.

Even though such considerations influence the quality of the service, the need for public providers to arrange the requirements of all the individuals they must serve means each member of the public cannot necessarily receive the service in the manner he or she would ultimately prefer. Public schooling implies an obligation to ensure all students are appropriately served. Finally, public schools teach skills business owners find very useful like competition, obedience, and respect for authority.

Charter Schools

A charter school is a public school of choice operating under the terms of a charter, or contract, with an authorizer, such as a state or local board of education. Charter schools receive flexibility from certain state and local rules in exchange for a higher degree of accountability for raising student achievement. Charter schools are held accountable by their authorizer(s) for upholding the terms of their charter. Charter schools are public schools. As such, they receive public funding, cannot charge tuition, must have fair and open enrollment, must be secular, and are required to serve all student populations, including students with disabilities and English language learners.

In the 1980s, the first charter schools are set up in Minnesota. As originally conceived, the ideal model of a charter school was a legally and financially autonomous public school (without tuition, religious affiliation, or selective student admissions) that would operate much like a private business—free from many state laws and district regulations, and accountable more for student outcomes rather than for processes or inputs (such as teacher certification requirements).

Flexibility and autonomy distinguish charter schools from traditional public schools. Charter schools are governed, not by a local board of education, but by an autonomous nonprofit board of directors. Charter schools use this flexibility to implement innovative or unique programs to provide educational options to parents and students not typically available in the traditional public schools. Charter schools are public schools of choice. Unlike private schools, they receive public funding, cannot charge tuition, and are not allowed to have admissions criteria. Also unlike private schools, charter schools are subject to many of the same state and federal regulations as traditional public schools. For example, charter schools participate in the same statewide assessments and accountability measures as traditional public schools.

Private Schools

Private schools (sometimes known as nonpublic or day schools) exist in the United States as corporate entities separate from public schools, which are supported by the government. Though they differ widely in function, geographical location, size, organizational pattern, and means of control, these schools have two features in common—they are ordinarily under the immediate control of a private corporation (religious or nonaffiliated), not of a government agency or board; and they are supported primarily by private funds. Parents select these schools for their children.

There are three main types of private schools: Catholic, other religious or parochial schools, or nonsectarian. Non-Catholic religious or parochial schools can be affiliated with any religion and is a school providing religious education in addition to conventional education. Nonsectarian schools do not have a religious orientation or purpose and are categorized into regular, special emphasis, and special education schools. Regular schools are those that have a regular elementary/secondary or early childhood program emphasis. Special emphasis schools are those that have, for example, a Montessori, vocational/technical, alternative, or special program emphasis. Special education schools are those that are designed to work with students with disabilities.

Private schools have been around for many years, and work to meet the needs of a wide range of students. Historically, private schools are thought to be only for rich or well-off students, but they also meet the needs of families desiring a religious education, for students who have special needs (either academically or socially), or for parents wanting something different from that provided by the local public school.

Private schools started in the United States as Catholic schools in the Deep South in the sixteenth century. Public and private schools worked closely together to provide educational services in many parts of the country. After the Civil War, there was a lot of animosity against private schools, accusing them of being un-American. This, in addition to anti-Catholic prejudice caused the closure of many schools across the United States. The influence of private schools waxed and waned over the next few decades. After World War II there was a dramatic increase in private schools, with numerous court cases supporting the use of public funds for private education—with limits, however. Private schools continued to flourish, but are affected by the rise and fall in economic stability of families.

The potential benefits of private schools accrue from their independence. Private schools do not receive tax revenues, so they do not have to follow the same sorts of regulations and bureaucratic processes governing public and charter schools. This allows many private schools to be highly specialized, offering differentiated learning, advanced curriculum, or programs geared toward specific religious beliefs.

In contrast to public schools, private schools must generate their own funding, which typically comes as tuition, private grants, and/or fund-raising from parents, alumni, and other community members. If the school is associated with a religious group, the local branch may provide an important source of funding as well.

Private Tutors

Long used in providing education to upper-class students over the centuries, private tutoring involves an instructor who gives individual lessons or apprenticeships. Private tutoring provides additional instruction to what occurs in either public or private schools, and is also referred to as shadow education. Private tutoring can help students excel in subject matter, and can also help students who are behind to keep up with their classmates. Private tutors are often paid for by the family, and as a sole means of providing education, can have very high costs.

Historically the sole form of education for upper-class families, private tutors have a rich and varied history. They have been providing individualized services for academic and social improvement, and also individual therapy for students with disabilities. Parents have hired them to help tutor for tests, finish papers, and to help with organization. It used to be that the private tutor was used in place of

formal education; now the private tutor is typically used to supplement or extend formal education. The separateness that used to exist is not really a big part of the educational picture.

The purpose, as mentioned above, is to provide intensive services at the student's level to either have them excel or to work to bring them up to the level of the other students. Intensive one-on-one instruction is also used to either supplant or supplement education provided in schools.

Homeschooling

Homeschooling involves the education of children in the home, either from parents or tutors. Formal schooling for many years was only available to upper-class students, and therefore the parents typically did all the education provided for others. Since the 1850s, most children are now educated in the schools. Homeschooling has increased in the last decade as an alternative to formal educational programs in either public or private schools. To provide an education to the student in a home-based setting based on the student's individual needs and the families interests and background. This allows the child to spend more time with their family, free from peer pressure, have parents as role models, and allows students to progress at their own rate.

Magnet Schools

These are public schools with specialized curriculums that draw students from across one school system, district, or corporation.

University Administered or Laboratory Schools

These are schools that operate in association with a college, university, or teacher education institution for training future teachers, educational research, and experimentation, as well as professional development efforts.

Climate of Competition

Numerous educators have weighed in on the topic of competition in education. One of the most notable is Diane Ravitch, who played a critical role in implementing competitive practices in the educational market, but has recently changed her perspective and is now anti-competition. When discussing her "change of heart" Ravitch shared, "The only way, then, to judge a school is by its intangibles—good schools have a strong culture of collaboration, with teachers working as a team to better their students" (Chicago Tonight, 2012). While Berkeley's Roger J. Traynor Professor of Law, Stephen B. Sugarman (2000), supports school choice on humanitarian grounds and describes one of the perceived positive effects of competition as community and family loyalty. He shared, "When families choose a private school today, they identify with the school in a way that is different from families who passively accept the school to which they are assigned. This choice-created commitment translates into an active loyalty that schools can draw upon in demanding the best from their families."

Whether you are supportive of school choice efforts or not, administrators in public schools no longer have time to debate the impending effects. It is now time to respond and examine how your programming and systems need to be adjusted in order to grow your school. In the upcoming chapter, we will discuss the impact of *Price* from a marketing perspective on public schools.

Chapter 5—Spotlight: Excel Centers

If your entire student population more than doubled between mid July and August would your school be prepared for the first day of classes? This is exactly the problem Scott Bess, Senior Vice President, Education & Chief Operating Officer for Goodwill Education Initiatives, Inc. and his staff found themselves in after opening their first Excel Center. The Excel Centers are tuition-free public charter schools that offer a credit recovery curriculum which provide students who have previously dropped out of high school a second chance to earn a high school diploma and additional certificates. In 2012–2013, the Excel Center in Anderson, was honored as a Four Star School by the state of Indiana. There are now nine Excel Centers across the state with a growing list of alumni.

The growth and subsequent success that the Excel Centers are currently experiencing is not the result of an amazing advertising campaign. In fact, before opening their third school, they had not advertised their services at all, but still had a waitlist. How can this be in such a competitive climate? When asked this question directly, Scott's answer is brilliantly simple, "we are really good at seeing a need and filling it."

The Excel Centers take a different approach to public education. Their ultimate goal is to attack poverty via education. They believe that graduation is only part of this journey. They focus their work on ensuring that students are ready to enter the workforce and that they are successful in achieving their dreams. When reviewing statewide drop out data, they found staggering numbers and density patterns. Below are a few of the key factors that were considered prior to opening their school in Anderson:

1.   Anderson needed us. The city of Anderson, IN, had once been a thriving suburb of Indianapolis that relied heavily on the automotive industry for jobs. Most of these jobs did not require a high school diploma. When the automotive industry moved out of Anderson, it left behind large numbers of the population with no high school diplomas and no job opportunities on

the horizon. Community wide poverty ran rampant; their city did not have the capacity to handle the systemic issues that began emerging.

2. Logistics. Anderson was an easy drive from their flagship school and central offices in Indianapolis.

3. Data Analysis. Excel looked specifically at districts that have numerous consecutive years (or decades) of producing high school dropouts.

4. Be practical and pragmatic. It has to be a good deal for everyone. We need to be able to find facilities that are widely accessible to the community and still meet our budgetary needs.

5. Community building first. We want to be liked and welcomed in a community. We focus on building a relationship with the community and we work with their existing traditional public schools prior to opening a school.

6. Will there be jobs for our graduates? We want to make sure our students are successful and a big part of that is making sure that we build a school in an area where it AND its graduates can be successful after they get a diploma. Is the community as dedicated to rebuilding as our students?

Questions

1. How do the Excel Centers push your thinking around product placement and schools?
2. In what ways has the Excel Center responded to a systemic issue and community need?
3. How can Excel's plan be revised to meet the needs of your school and community?

Applying the Concepts

1. When you examine your internal value chain, where do you see strengths and opportunities to grow?
2. When you examine your school's external value chain, where do you see strengths and opportunities to grow?

References

Martin, R. (2010). The execution trap. *Harvard Business Review.* Retrieved from http://hbr.org/2010/07/the-execution-trap/ar/1.

Stern, L. and El-Ansary, A. (1982). *Marketing Channels,* (2nd ed.). Englewood Cliffs, NJ: Prentice-Hall.

Sugarman, S. (2000). http://www.law.berkeley.edu/faculty/sugarmans/congressmonthly.htm

http://www.law.berkeley.edu/faculty/sugarmans/congressmonthly.htm

http://hbr.org/2008/07/putting-the-service-profit-chain-to-work

Chapter 6

Price

We cannot go out and raise the price of our product to assist us covering this. We would have to go to the taxpayers and ask for some type of increase, and I just don't see that happening.

—Les Huddle, Superintendent Lafayette (IN) School Corporation

In most cases, price is at the heart of the value exchange. It quantifies the value the Consumer must give up in order to acquire the item of value they desire in return. For an organization, Pricing strategy is extremely important, as it is the only element in the marketing mix that generates revenue. Pricing strategy is complex and involves not only an intricate understanding of the firm's production costs and its revenue goals, but a solid grasp on a variety of external economic factors, including competition and demand, as well as behavioral variables such as consumer perception. Most organizations consider a variety of pricing strategies and engage in extensive analysis to forecast the impact on sales of different pricing models. Given that public education is not tuition-based, this book will not engage in a lengthy discussion of pricing strategies. Rather, we will provide a basic framework of pricing strategies and use this framework as a guide to discuss how consumers interpret price as a measure of value.

Pricing strategy is a function of the product's position, as well as its stage in the product life cycle. Organizations will carefully forecast the movement in price as a product moves through the cycle. Figure 6.1 demonstrates options for pricing of new products.

FIGURE 6.1—New Product Pricing Strategies

Products utilizing Price Skimming set a high initial price as a means of skimming as much revenue as possible from each layer of the market (Armstrong & Kotler, 2013). Firms set an initial high price when the product is introduced and is perceived to have unique advantages. This strategy generally works only when consumers are willing to buy the product even though it carries an above-average price tag. As the firm enters the growth and maturity stages of the life cycle, when competition increases, the price is generally lowered. At the other end of the continuum is Penetration Pricing. Firms pursuing this strategy set a low price as a way to reach out to a mass market. This strategy is designed to capture large market shares, which will contribute to lower production costs as a result of the firm realizing economies of scale. Products with few, if any, unique points of differentiation typically utilize penetration Pricing. Unlike Price Skimming, which encourages competition, the low price point utilized in Penetration Pricing typically discourages competition. Other firms try to avoid pricing wars by simply setting prices in line with competition. Also referred to as Going Rate Pricing, Status Quo Pricing is simple to implement, though it tends to ignore demand or production costs. Typically this strategy is employed in competitive market places.

Once the base price for a product is established, a firm will implement any number of price adjustment strategies to react to the competitive environment. Options range from discounts and promotional pricing, to geographic and psychological pricing. However, as we have previously stated, this chapter will not provide an extensive discussion of pricing strategies, given that public schools do not charge a price to Consumers who use the service.

The chief thing to remember is the pricing strategy selected by the firm should support the overall positioning of the product. Positioning is the guiding factor for all aspects of the marketing mix and pricing is no different. The cost to produce a generic brand golf shirt sold at a discount store is not that much different from the production costs for a status brand, such as Ralph Lauren or Lacoste. However, consumers are willing to pay far more for the latter shirt because they associate a much higher level of status with them than they do with the generic shirt. The utilitarian, functional value of both shirts is the same—they cover up a person's torso and arms. However, the perceived social benefits to the consumer go beyond any practical purpose. To some, the shirt may have been purchased as a means of letting others know the consumer could afford to purchase a higher priced brand. To others, the shirt serves as a signal the consumer has good fashion sense. As we reviewed in Chapter Two, there are any number of factors, both external and internal, affecting a consumer's

MichaelJayBerlin/Shutterstock.com

purchase decision. In the case of schools, parents' decisions related to where they send their children to school—be it public or private—can be related to everything from a desire to project their status in the community to a reflection of their personal or faith-based values.

Value is What You Get

As Warren Buffet stated, "Price is what you pay. Value is what you get." This quote gets to the root of marketing—the value exchange. However, as we have stated, in most cases, the consumer is giving up something of value—typically money—to receive something of value in return—a haircut or a new pair of shoes, for example. Even in cases of not-for-profits, there is a value exchange; the consumer gives up volunteer hours and receives a good feeling in return. On the most basic level, the value exchange for public education is quite similar. Parents pay taxes to support a public school system, in exchange for which they have the opportunity to have their children receive an education. This way of looking at the education value exchange supports the marketing model we proposed in Chapter One—with the school system serving as the Producer or Seller and Families as the Buyers or Consumers, as depicted in the image below.

On a deeper level, however, it is easy to see that the essence of the value exchange for public education is rooted much more in the Education Value Chain introduced in Chapter Five. If the public school remains the Producer or Seller, the Value on the Micro-level is exchanged with families. However, families alone do not fund the purchase; rather, the community at-large supports the educational system through their taxes. Likewise, the community ultimately receives the benefits of an educated populace. Thus, on a Macro-level, it becomes clear the Producer or Seller is the public school system and the Buyer or Consumer is the community as a whole. Adopting this wider view, we would argue the public school systems, without knowing it, were actually one of the first industries to practice the Societal Marketing Concept—that of meeting the Buyer's needs in a way benefiting not only the consumer but society as well. While this may seem an obvious point for educators, we would further argue it is something that is often overlooked by many public schools—or one touted only during a referendum campaign. However, the value exchange between schools and the community occurs every day and schools should not dismiss the community as a stakeholder audience.

FIGURE 6.2—Public School Value Exchange

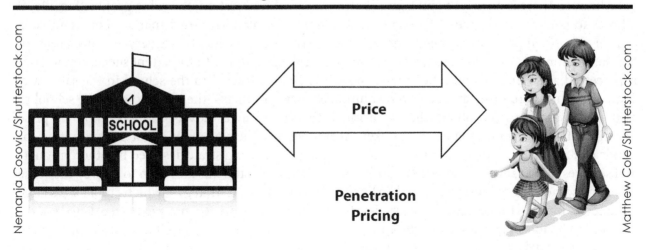

Every stakeholder group the school serves should understand the value delivered by public schools—and it is the school's responsibility to make it known. At the higher education level, public colleges and universities do not hesitate to issue reports on the public good they provide—including their social, educational, and economic impact. When seeking legislative support, these institutions readily point to the impact of their operations and the contributions of their students and alumni as a means of demonstrating the overall value they provide—not just to individual students but also to the communities and states where they operate.

As we have stated, a product's pricing strategy is driven by its value proposition. While public schools can—and should—adopt a competitive position—they will never be called on to tie that positioning to an actual price point. Public education is a public industry product, paid for and supported by the public. Unlike private-industry products, whose success depends on the ability to meet consumers' needs better than their competitors, public education is driven by public entities—taxpayers, lawmakers, and the like. However, faced with increasing competition, identifying and communicating the value proposition delivered has never been more vital for public schools.

Although there is no price point being charged for public education, the value proposition allows schools to convey the degree of the value exchange to the intended target market. For example, a charter school emphasizing a math and science curriculum will identify a very narrow target of families wishing to stress those subjects in their children's educations. To the extent such a curriculum is perceived as so unique and different, consumers may be attracted to the school in the same way some consumers are easily attracted to revolutionary new products—thereby allowing the school to skim away students from other schools, in much the same way as novel products employ a price skimming tactic when they enter the market. Again, because the consumer is not paying tuition for public education, it is difficult to make exact parallels to the pricing strategies used by other products and services. For example, schools that target a mass volume of students and wish to convey the sense of having something for everyone could be likened to a penetration strategy—which emphasizes large volume. However, while a penetration pricing strategy can easily work for many mass-marketed goods, we caution schools against conveying a mass appeal value message. As we have stated previously, the pricing models and techniques employed by private industry do not apply to a public industry

YuryZap/Shutterstock.com

product like education. Nonetheless, we do hold tight to the notion that the lack of a price tag does not mean that no value is being exchanged. On the contrary, public schools deliver tremendous value—in exchange for many things, such as the time, effort, and interest of students and parents, as well as the tax support, good will, and hopefully feeling of pride from the community in which the school operates.

School Choice and School Finance

While public schools may not be able to impact the price of their product, their budgets have certainly been impacted by school choice. The ripple effects of school choice have caused monumental change to school finance. For years, public schools have not had to think about competition, market share, or how their costs were perceived in comparison to others. They were the only place in town where students could be educated, and in some rural areas that still exists. However, there have been significant changes to funding for public schools and competition is here and it is important. While public schools may not be able to impact the price of their products, their budgets have certainly been impacted by school choice. The ripple effects of school choice have caused monumental change to school finance. There are different types of school choice, understanding each will help public school administrators appreciate the effect they have on schools.

Though there have been variation on school choice for the past fifty years, the school choice took a substantial step forward with the nation's first publicly financed urban school choice program, the Milwaukee Parental Choice Program. Several similar initiatives were established in the years following; utilizing both the voucher and the tax credit model, with publicly funded and supported choice programs developing in Arizona, Florida, Minnesota, Pennsylvania, and Ohio. Numerous organizations were established to help support school choice. The US Supreme Court added further credibility to the school choice movement with a decision in *Zelman v. Simmons-Harris* (2002). In

that decision the Court provided a framework to help guide and understand school choice: (1) the program must have a valid secular purpose; (2) aid must go to parents and not to the schools; (3) a broad class of beneficiaries must be covered; (4) the program must be neutral with respect to religion; and (5) there must be adequate nonreligious options.

The main different types of school choice include vouchers, tuition tax credits, charter schools, magnet schools, and open enrollment. Each has changed the way we think about financing of public schools.

Vouchers

A school voucher is a certificate provided by the public school which a parent can use toward the tuition at a private school or use to help defray the costs of homeschooling. Vouchers are intended to help parents make a choice about where their child is to attend school. The parents still pay taxes into the system, but are given the opportunity to take the money that would have been used to educate their child and take that to a private school. One of the funding controversies regarding the use of vouchers is shifting a handful of students from a public school into private schools will not decrease what the public school must pay for teachers and facilities, but funding for those costs will decrease as students leave.

Tuition Tax Credits

Depending on the state, parents may deduct a portion of the tuition paid for education-related expenses at nonpublic schools. These expenses can include tuition, after-school programs, tutoring, educational camps, and other related expenses. The tuition tax credits can be for private nonprofit schools, in addition to public schools in different districts. There are numerous controversies related to the use of tuition tax credits including debates surrounding the separation of church and state, but one of the biggest problems with tuition tax credits is students moving from public to private schools harms school districts because they cannot reduce their fixed facilities and transportation costs in proportion to the number of students who leave.

Charter Schools

For a greater description of the history and purpose of charter schools, please see Chapter Five, Place. However, defining charter schools is difficult because state laws that govern them are so different. However, charter schools generally share three characteristics: (1) They are public schools—free to attend, publicly funded, part of the state school system, and accountable for their results; (2) They are schools of choice, parents can choose to send their children to these schools without restrictions of residency; (3) They are privately managed by an organization that has a charter, or contract. Similar to the financing problems associated with vouchers and tuition tax credits, the effect of charter schools on public school funding is shifting a handful of students from a public school into charter schools will not decrease what the public school must pay for teachers, facilities, and transportation, but funding for those costs will decrease as students leave.

Magnet Schools

Magnet schools are public schools that take students regardless of school boundaries or specific curriculum. Depending on the magnet school, students can come from other parts of the school district, or from neighboring districts. A popular option is the school within a school magnet that is a part of a larger school but providing specialized services or programming for a select group of the students. Types of magnet schools include specialized programs in mathematics, humanities, performing arts, or vocational education. These programs help meet the diversified needs of students and provide them enrichment in their areas of interest while still in school. The controversy for funding magnet schools as a part of public school financing is the same as for vouchers, tuition tax credits, and charter schools. The costs of providing basic transportation, heating, computer, library, counseling services for the students who are not a part of the magnet school and stay with the public school is a fairly fixed cost and is necessary to meet those students' needs even after the other students have left.

Open Enrollment

Open enrollment allows a student to transfer to the public school of his or her choice. There are two basic types of open-enrollment policies: intra-district and inter-district. Intra-district open-enrollment policies allow a student to transfer to another school within his or her school district. Inter-district open enrollment allows a student to transfer to a school outside his or her home district, but often requires both the sending district and the receiving district to agree to participate. Some states have policies allowing districts to choose whether to participate depending on available space.

Transportation costs are typically the responsibility of a parent or guardian, school district, or other entity. Like the other forms of school choice discussed, costs for students not participating in the switching of schools are fixed, and the school may lose money with a few students leaving.

Family and Community Engagement in the Era of School Choice

Keeping up with educational policy and reform in recent years has been almost impossible for even the most seasoned veteran. On a very regular basis, the profession of education is discussed as part of local, national, and international platforms. Essentially, everyone discussing or impacting the field of education today is a former consumer of education and, in some cases, a current school shopper.

Whether you were educated at home, in a public school, or a private school, an overwhelming percent of our populace has some experience with education. It's not often that a product is as widely experienced by the populace as education. In many ways, the overall structure of school has changed very little in the last 50 years and many people have opinions and perspectives about education based on personal experience (Fowler, 2004). Even more pointed on the topic of the connection between community experience and education was Abraham Lincoln. He is believed to have said, "The philosophy of the school room in one generation will be the philosophy of the government in the next."

As one of the first practitioners of the societal marketing concept, public schools—whose overarching premise has been to sustain our society—must now evolve in order to sustain themselves. In recent years, educational research efforts have been focused on who is and is not achieving. In the mainstream media, countless outlets discuss the success and failures, as well as the expense of public education. From a more cyclical perspective, public opinion drives public education and public education ends up driving the public opinion of future generations. If the theories of the societal marketing concept holds true, then public schools must not only provide a student with an exceptional educational experience, they must also be viewed favorably by taxpayers. This is why all of the feel-good stories about one district on the news will never be enough, if the overall opinion of public education in the same area is dismal. Public schools must be seen as serving a larger public good. As we have discussed in previous chapters, the mission and purpose of public education has evolved throughout our country's history; today's changes are far more focused on structure and results. To market your public school from a societal marketing concept, you must have a dynamic understanding of your community. It is important to assert that it is not what you believe your community needs from public schools, it is what they tell you and show you.

Much of the previous work on family and community engagement has been written prior to school choice movements. It pushed educators to work with families and community partners as a way to increase student achievement and provided strategies of best practice. In the era of school choice, parent trigger laws, and vouchers, family and community engagement is no longer a recommended best practice; it is a required practice for sustainability. We have mountains of data to tell us who is achieving and who is not, as well as which students are being treated equitably and which ones are not. Additionally, public schools also know who are their supporters and who are not based on the voting patterns, public comments, philanthropic support, and mainstream media coverage they receive. All of this is important data for public schools to assess. If there are large groups of students not achieving or being treated inequitably in your public school, it is safe to assume that those students and families are not satisfied with the educational experience your school is providing. Further, these dissatisfied families represent a potential loss for your school, as they look more seriously at their competitive options.

Educational issues that have formerly been couched as social justice, are no longer about ethics. Now they are about economics. Today's unhappy families and communities are tomorrow's school shoppers. Rather than taking a defensive approach to negative feedback, public schools need to authentically listen to their communities. Smiley, Howland, and Anderson (2008) found one public district was offering services based on what they believed families wanted, rather than asking families what they needed. This led to poor attendance at school events.

When interviewed about the lack of family engagement in light of numerous attempts, school officials believed the community did not value education. Conversely, families interviewed did not feel valued by the school because the school was not attempting to meet their needs. Both parties were wrong and the victims of "communication only" marketing efforts. In the years following this research, the school system faced insurmountable public backlash, large numbers of publicly supported charters, and subsequent departure of a crippling number of students. As students left, so did the public funding and vouchers they brought with them.

As we have discussed, Price for public schools does not represent what is being charged, as it does with private sector goods and services. However, just because no tuition is being assessed does not mean that a value exchange is not occurring. The value exchange is considerable—at both the student and community levels. Pricing strategy for retail goods and services considers both the cost of production as well as the overall product's positioning. Clearly, public educators understand the rising production costs associated with providing a student with an educational experience and that every lost student represents real dollars the school is not bringing to its bottom line. What is most important for educators to consider is that, in this unprecedented age of educational choice and competition, schools must continue to understand and meet the needs of all their stakeholders in order to remain competitive and successful.

Chapter 6—SPOTLIGHT: Junction City

In July of 2009, the state department of education notified Junction City, a small Midwestern public school district on the fringe of a large urban area, that their new funding formula would include reduced funds in 2010 and 2011 and major reductions in 2012. The school is racially diverse and almost 60% of their student population receives free or reduced lunch services. Given the devastating news that they were facing crippling budget cuts, the district level administrative team decided to develop a bond referendum plan focused on three major components: Financial Realities, Legal Contexts, and Political Action. Within each category they brainstormed what had taken place in the past, as well as what they needed to do for a fiscally sound future. They also designated which pieces would require the support of outside consultants. Their action plan details were as follows:

Financial Realities

- ► Work begins 24–36 months before receiving funds
- ► Normal projection is 18 months
- ► Referendum projection at least 24 months and best at 36 months
- ► Document past revenue and state support accurately
- ► Estimate future revenue and state support conservatively
- ► Document past expenses accurately
- ► Estimate future expenses liberally
- ► Reduce expenses in all areas—document these reductions
- ► Plan for and accept additional reductions
- ► Document past net assessed value (Consultant Needed)
- ► Document past tax levies and rates
- ► Estimate future assessed value (Consultant Needed)
- ► Estimate revenue necessary from the referendum (Consultant Needed)
- ► Estimate expenses charged to referendum (Consultant Needed)
- ► Estimate referendum rate and revenue (Consultant Needed)

Legal

- ▶ Work begins 6–12 months before the referendum
- ▶ Legal consultation needed regarding all legal matters
- ▶ Create a Timetable
- ▶ Local Resolution, Minutes, and Certification
- ▶ County Policies and Rules
- ▶ County Resolution
- ▶ State Code—Referendum Tax Levy
- ▶ State Code—Local Public Questions

Political

- ▶ Work begins 12–24 months before the referendum
- ▶ What does the public think about your schools?
- ▶ What does the public know about your schools?
- ▶ What does the public see about your schools?
- ▶ What does the public value about your schools?
- ▶ Do you really know the answers to these questions?
- ▶ How can we learn to answer these questions? (professional assistance)
- ▶ We are now in a political campaign, this has little to do with our profession . . . accept this
- ▶ We need a political action committee
- ▶ The public needs to experience, in some manner, what school will be like without the funds
- ▶ Identify the source of the issue—early and often
- ▶ Be positive about all things school-related
- ▶ Communication with/and education of the adult audience becomes paramount
- ▶ Media—electronic, personal, print
- ▶ What not to do . . .
  - • Highly visible construction projects
  - • Protracted negotiations calling attention to salaries and benefits
  - • High profile school administration

Timeline of Activities

- ▶ July 2009—New funding formula—reduced revenue in 2010, 2011, and a major reduction in 2012
- ▶ July 2009—Long Term Revenue vs. Expenses developed to illustrate issues in 2012
- ▶ July 2009—Narrative of causes of revenue issues developed
- ▶ August 2009—School opened with large classes to demonstrate the future
- ▶ August 2009—Families come forward asking for smaller classes and agreeing to participate in efficiency plan that will result in reduced spending in 2010–2011
- ▶ September 2009—Efficiency Committee forms and meets and attempts to identify ways to reduce expenses by 20% by 2012
- ▶ October 2009—Efficiency Committee determines that expenses cannot be reduced inside the current school structure and that a change in structure was unacceptable. Efficiency Committee determines that revenue must be increased.

- November 2009—Efficiency Committee recommends pursuit of referendum to the School Board
- December 2009—The School Board hears a report from the legal counsel regarding a referendum to the School Board
- January 2010—School Board adopts resolution to conduct a referendum
- January 2010—Referendum Steering Committee Formed
- February 2010—Clint City–County Council acknowledges the referendum
- February 2010—Campaign Begins Professional poll of resident Junction City voters. The results of this poll inform all future communications
- February 2010—Letter to the Editor Campaign Begins
- February 2010—Websites Established
- February 2010—Electronic letters, blogs, and Facebook pages begin
- February 2010—Public presentations begin
- March 2010—All February communication above continues. Public meetings are important, they represent personal service
- March 2010—Get-Out the Vote Planning Begins
- April 2010—Early voting and absentee voting publicized and utilized
- April 2010—Yard signs distributed (do not gain votes, but secure votes, and discourage opposition)
- April 2010—Door-to-door canvassing of neighborhoods by parents and teachers
- April 2010—Direct Mail—Important to voters who do not use electronic media
- April 2010—Phone calls continue—used to create a list of supporters, which will then be used on Election Day
- May 2010—Public Rally—Keep up enthusiasm
- May 2010—Election Day—over 100 volunteers to serve at covering every polling location

More than 60% of this school's community qualifies for free and reduced lunch support. This community has a reputation for being very fiscally conservative and this vote took place while the community was trying to recover from a national recession. Junction City has a large population of elderly residents, who no longer have children that are school aged. Additionally, this is a traditional public school, in a climate when much of the public discourse about public education is negative. Seemingly, all of the cards were stacked against this school, but they developed and implemented a comprehensive and purposeful marketing plan. By following this plan, Junction City secured a referendum bond that was 3 times more than the previous amount and it passed with more than 85% of residents voting yes.

Questions

1. Which aspects of the promotional mix did Junction City utilize in their referendum plan?
2. In what ways did the district level administration anticipate and respond to the needs of their community?
3. How can this plan be revised for other schools navigating different issues? What portions of this plan could be considered universal? What portions could be considered specific for this school and situation?

Applying the Concepts

1. Prepare a chart with five sections: Advertising, Public Relations, Personal Selling, Sales Promotion, and Direct Marketing. Put the various promotional activities of Junction City in the correlating categories.
2. Write a summary of how each aspect of the promotional mix was utilized to reach Junction City's end goal.
3. What is a need your school may have that could be met by the promotional mix?
4. Develop a second chart outlining your ideas of how to utilize the promotional mix to reach your end goal.

References

Armstrong, G., & Kotler, P. (2013). *Marketing: An Introduction* (11th ed.). Boston, MA: Pearson.

Fowler, F. C. (2004). *Policy studies for educational leaders: An introduction.* Upper Saddle River, NJ: Pearson.

Smiley, A. D., Howland, A. A, & Anderson, J. A. (2008). Cultural brokering as a core practice of a special education parent liaison program in a large urban school district. *Journal of Urban Learning, Teaching and Research.* Los Angeles, CA: American Educational Research Association. 4, 86–95.

http://www.indystar.com/article/20130606/NEWS05/306060078/Some-schools-trim-part-time-hours-avoid-Obamacare-requirements.

Chapter 7

Promotion

What really decides consumers to buy or not to buy
is the content of your advertising, not its form.

—*David Ogilvy,* "The Father of Advertising."

The final P of the marketing mix—Promotion—is undoubtedly the aspect of the marketing mix with which consumers are most familiar. Promotion includes the various means through which the organization attempts to "inform, persuade, and remind consumers—directly or indirectly—about the products and brands they sell" (Kotler & Keller, 2012). Also referred to as the Promotion mix, this aspect of the marketing mix includes its own set of tools, including Advertising, Public Relations, Personal Selling, Sales Promotion, and Direct Marketing. In this chapter, we will review the components of the Promotion mix and how organizations use these communication tools to help achieve their marketing objectives. First, we will briefly review the cultural and technological changes that have resulted in a shift in the manner in which organizations implement their marketing communications strategies.

Prior to the evolution of the Internet and the digital age, the flow of communication from organizations to their customers was predominantly one-directional. To use a simplified description of the communications process—a company would develop a message and send it through a selected media channel to the receiver who interprets the message. However, the standard communication process, as outlined here, also allows for opportunities for feedback from the receiver back to the message sender. For example, in the case of direct, face-to-face communication, the receiver can provide immediate verbal and visual feedback. However, when indirect communication such as advertising is employed, the receiver cannot provide direct, immediate feedback to the message sender. In other words, if a consumer does not understand the content of an advertiser's commercial, the company has no way of collecting that immediate feedback.

With the evolution of the Internet and social media, the communication landscape has shifted to a model, which now permits the full participation of consumers in dialog related to companies and

Twin Design/Shutterstock.com

brands. These technologies not only enable consumers to be better informed, but they facilitate the exchange of information with companies and—perhaps more importantly—with other consumers. Social media, blogs, and websites afford consumers tremendous resources to share information about their product experiences.

Technology has also impacted the messaging strategies organizations are using to promote their products. Sophisticated databases and the ability to track online behavior have given marketers the tools to move their messaging strategy from single-message broadcasting to customized-message narrowcasting (Armstrong & Kotler, 2013). In addition, marketers are joining consumers online, creating brand affinity communities on social networks and even utilizing other consumers to help create and share messages. In the latter strategy, referred to as buzz marketing, organizations enlist influential consumers or other opinion leaders to serve as ambassadors for the product; these envoys help spread the brand message using their own words and opinions. The goal of this persuasive form of communication is to increase both awareness of as well as affinity for the brand. In fact, one study found buzz marketing programs can increase word of mouth marketing by as much as 50% (Business Wire, 2010).

As a result of the increased technology and consumer involvement, marketers have shifted their emphasis on mass communication and have begun to look at the overall impact the use of all of their promotional tools has on consumers. For example, a product advertising message may state one thing, while a website or direct mail promotion may say something else, and an in-store salesperson may convey yet another impression. In response, marketers have moved to develop a more unified approach to their marketing communication planning process. Integrated marketing communication seeks to track all of the points where consumers may come into contact with a company and all its brands and messages, for the purpose of delivering an overall streamlined, consistent message and creating a positive image for the organization. To do this, the organization must have a solid understanding of the strengths and weaknesses of each tool in the Promotion mix, as well as the media channels through which marketing messages can be sent. In the next sections, we will address the various aspects of the Promotion Mix.

Advertising

Advertising helps an organization communicate the value proposition. Advertising can be defined as "the development and dissemination of messages by any sponsoring organization or individual designed to inform or persuade a target audience about a particular product, service or idea." The key is to understand the sender of the message has decision control over both the message content and the media selected to convey the message. The key is to understand the sender of the message has decision control over both the message content and the media selected to convey the message.

As a promotional tool, advertising offers both strengths and weaknesses. For the advertiser, advertising allows a single brand message to be conveyed to numerous consumers at once. Depending on the medium selected, advertisers can employ any number of creative techniques to communicate the message. However, because consumers recognize the advertiser is in control of the message, there is often some skepticism among buyers relative to the reliability of the claims being made in an ad. Further, due to the fact that most mass mediums reach a large audience—combined with the fact that advertising airtime or space is priced based on the size of the audience delivered—advertising, as a promotional tool, is generally very expensive.

Because paid advertising consists not only of the message content but media selection, it is important for marketers to have a good understanding of the effective value of various forms of media. The table below provides a brief overview of the strengths and weaknesses of various forms of media.

TABLE 7.1—Media Strengths and Weaknesses

Media	Strengths	Weaknesses
Television	High reach—delivers large audiences Low cost per impression High intrusion value and credibility Numerous creative messaging options and production techniques Audience segmentation options available through varied programs	Clutter—from total number of advertisers Low recall Increased competition Channel surfing, DVR usage—means ads could be overlooked Short exposure time (typically :30) Due to large audience reached, large budgets required
Radio	Easily targeted audience, due to station format Creative flexibility and low cost Delivers local audience Mobile medium	Short exposure time (typically :60) Low attention levels Increased competition from other audio sources

Media	Strengths	Weaknesses
Outdoor	Geographic targeting Accessible for local ads High reach Low cost per impression High frequency on major commuter routes Creative flexibility	Short exposure time Creative limitations Little audience segmentation possible
Magazines	Easily targeted audience, due to editorial format High color quality Long shelf life Longer attention to ad Credible Tangible	Declining readership High level of clutter Long lead time to ad showing Little flexibility High cost
Newspaper	Local audience delivery High flexibility Credible Tangible Longer message possible Coupons or inserts possible	Short shelf life Clutter from total number of advertisers Poor production quality Declining readership
Digital	Creative possibilities Short lead time to send ad Simplicity of target segmentation High audience interest Excellent measurement metrics Numerous options—search, display, mobile, games, social, banner ads	Clutter from other advertisers Difficult ad buying procedures Short life span Low intrusion value

(Calder, 2008; Clow & Baack, 2001)

Selecting the appropriate media for use in an advertising campaign is equally important to the proper development of the message itself. The media plan needs to consider the objective of the advertising campaign, the target audience and their media habits, the creative messaging strategy, as well as the budget.

FuzzBones/Shutterstock.com

Public Relations

The Public Relations Society of America (PRSA) defines Public Relations (PR) as "a strategic communication process that builds mutually beneficial relationships between organizations and their publics" (Copyright © Public Relations Society of America. Reprinted by permission. http://www. prsa.org/AboutPRSA/PublicRelationsDefined/). An organization's publics—sometimes referred to as stakeholders—includes internal and external groups. A stakeholder is an individual or group with a vested interest in the organization (Baack, 1997). The table below identifies different types of stakeholder groups.

TABLE 7.2—Stakeholder Groups

Internal Stakeholders	External Stakeholders
Employees	Channel members
Volunteers	Customers
Unions	Local community
Shareholders/Tax Payers	Financial community
Board members	Government
Retirees	Community organizations
Donors	Special-interest groups
Students	Media

Public relations seek to generate interest in or awareness of the organization, its products or events or issues. However, unlike advertising—PR seeks to cultivate this attention without paying for airtime or space. To do this, PR professionals serve a variety of functions in order to maintain positive relationships with stakeholder groups; these include the following:

Media Relations: The activities involved in working with the media to generate publicity for a product, service, or organization. This includes establishing contact with media reporters, providing publicity materials to media or other groups, and being available to answer any questions the media might have.

Product Publicity: The non-paid-for communication of information about the company or product, generally in some media format. This could include product placement in television or movies.

Public Affairs: The managerial function concerned with the relationships that exist between the organization and its external environment. Key tasks include intelligence gathering and analysis, internal communication, and any external initiatives directed at government, communities, or the general public.

Lobbying: A person or group of persons seeking to influence the proceedings or efforts of legislative bodies through personal intervention.

Investor Relations: Relationships built with company stockholders or investors, as well as others representatives who work in the financial community.

Development: Efforts by non-profits to build relationships with donors or other stakeholders to gain financial or volunteer support.

(AMA, 2013; Armstrong & Kotler, 2013).

A solid public relations strategy can be an effective part of the overall marketing plan because they can be used either to address the specific needs or concerns of a narrow audience or public (as in the case of employee relations) or they can be a cost-effective, expedient, and credible method for reaching out to a broad public (as in the case of media relations).

Personal Selling

Personal selling allows the organization to build customer relationships and generate sales through the use of face-to-face or other personalized presentations by the sales force (Armstrong & Kotler, 2013).

Depending on the size and structure of the organization, the customers to whom they sell and the type of products sold, the sales function will differ. Some organizations utilize inside salespeople—individuals whose job is to meet the needs of customers who contact the organization. Examples of inside sales positions can be found in retail settings to salespeople who accept inbound telephone orders. Often these individuals are referred to as order takers. Other organizations use outside salespeople—individuals whose job is to go out and meet clients or customers, identify their needs and suggest a product or service solution that will meet those needs. A wide range of examples of outside sales positions can be found in business-to-business sales including office equipment, heavy machinery, professional services, advertising, and many others. Examples of business-to-consumer outside sales positions can include financial services and home improvement services, among others. Generally, though there are exceptions, inside salespeople are compensated more heavily through an hourly or salary arrangement, while outside salespeople tend to be compensated through commissions, though some organizations use a combination of both to compensate their sales staff.

Organizations that include personal selling in their promotional mix generally understand that there are high costs associated with staffing, training, and supporting the sales force. With this in mind, the use of personal selling must be appropriate to the product or service being sold and the customer purchasing behavior. In other words, a consumer doesn't need the help of a sales representative to make a soda purchase from a convenience store or vending machine, although a sales representative can provide significant assistance to a buyer in the purchase of a car.

While many organizations utilize a selling process specific to their own industry or company, the sales process typically entails seven specific steps. They include:

Prospecting and qualifying—The steps involved in identifying and qualifying potential customers for the organization.

Pre-approach—The activities preceding the sales call where the salesperson collects as much information as possible about the prospect, prior to a meeting.

Approach—The initial stage in a sales interaction, when the salesperson meets the prospect for the first time. The objectives of the approach include building rapport with the prospect, gaining their attention and interest, and moving the relationship to the next phase of the selling process.

Presentation and/or demonstration—In this stage of the personal selling process, the salesperson transmits the information about the product and attempts to persuade the prospect to become a customer by demonstrating how the product or service being offered will solve the prospect's problem.

Handling objections—The actions of the salesperson to seek out, clarify, and overcome any questions or concerns raised by the prospect.

Closing—The culmination of a sales presentation in which a salesperson asks for the order or tries to confirm the sale.

Follow-up—The process of contacting the customer, after the sale, to ensure satisfaction, repeat business, or handle any subsequent questions or issues. Although the sale has occurred, the follow-up step is vital to the continuation of the relationship between the organization and the customer.

(AMA, 2013; Armstrong & Kotler, 2013).

An organization's use of personal selling can be an effective tool in helping the organization identify the specific needs of the buyer and carefully coordinate the resources of the company to create a customized solution to help meet those needs, and thereby build a lasting relationship with the customer.

Sales Promotion

Sales promotion encompasses the media and non-media marketing strategies—applied for a pre-determined, limited period of time—to consumers, retailers, or wholesalers in order to stimulate trial, increase consumer demand, or improve product availability (AMA, 2013). To clarify, sales promotion activities can be aimed at consumers or toward the marketing intermediaries. Consumer-oriented sales promotion activities are typically used to generate trial or sales, while sales promotion activities focused on retailers or wholesalers are designed to expand product distribution outlets. The AMA definition also makes reference to media and non-media strategies. This addresses the fact that a sales promotion strategy, such as a January White Sale, may utilize television advertising to communicate the sales offer to consumers. However, the short-term incentive designed to get consumers to come in and purchase bed linens is a sales promotional strategy, not an advertising strategy. To distinguish further, advertising refers to product awareness and information messaging, while sales promotion—even if communicated through a television commercial—refers to a short-term sale or incentive to purchase a product during a specific time period.

There are a number of tools marketers can use to accomplish their sales promotion objectives. The table below distinguishes consumer promotion tools, from industry and business promotion tools.

TABLE 7.3—Sales Promotion Tools

Consumer Promotions	
Samples	Offers of a trial amount of a product.
Coupons	Certificates that offer consumers a money savings on the purchase of a product.
Cash Refunds (Rebates)	Similar to coupons, except that the price discount occurs after the purchase, rather than at the time of purchase.
Price Packs (Cents-Off Deals)	A savings offer posted directly on the product. Can include a money-savings deal on a single product or a two-for-the-price-of-one discount.
Premiums	Additional goods that are offered either free or at a low cost as an incentive to purchase a product.
Advertising Specialties	Includes a wide range of promotional products imprinted with the product's name or message distributed to consumers.
Point-of-Purchase Promotions	Also referred to as POP. Includes displays or demonstrations at the place of sale.
Contests, Sweepstakes, and Games	Promotional activities that give consumers a chance at winning something. Contests call for consumers to submit an entry, which will be judged by a panel, who will select a winner. Sweepstakes select a winner through a random drawing among all the entrants. Games present consumers with a puzzle or number every time they make a purchase, which may or may not lead to a prize.
Events/sponsorships	Creating a brand-oriented event or supporting events created by others, for the purpose of increasing awareness of the brand or product.
Trade Promotions	
Discounts	Companys discount the sale of the product to the retailer as an inducement for them to carry the product. Retailers still sell the product to the consumer at the regular price, but increase their profit on the product during the period of the discount.
Allowances	Companys offer a per-case allowance on sales made during a period in which the retailer agrees to feature the product in the store, through advertising or in-store displays, for example.

Free Goods	Extra merchandise offered to retailers who agree to feature the product.
Push Money	Extra money or gifts offered to dealers to encourage their sales forces to "push" the manufacturer's products.
Business Promotions	
Conventions and Trade Shows	An exhibition or event in which manufactures display their products to retailers or distributors.
Sales Contests	A contest conducted for salespeople or dealers to motivate them to increase their sales performance over a particular period of time.

(Kotler & Keller, 2012)

Direct Marketing

Direct Marketing can be defined as "a form of non-store retailing which utilizes an impersonal medium, such as catalogs or direct response television ads, to communicate a product or service value proposition directly to consumers enabling them to purchase the offering." Similar to Sales Promotion, direct marketing also seeks an immediate response from the promotional effort. The evolution of communications options has afforded direct marketers to become more and more sophisticated in their methods of contacting prospects with their offers. Early direct marketing efforts were communicated through catalogs or other mailers; this later evolved to the use of telemarketing. Direct marketing efforts on television have also evolved significantly—moving from 30- and 60-second

commercials promoting record albums or books, to program-length infomercials and cable channels, like QVC and HSN, whose programming is fully centered around direct marketing. According to the Direct Marketing Association, in 2011, American companies spend nearly $155 billion per year on direct marketing efforts—a figure which was projected to grow each year (DMA, 2011).

Some consumers have historically been suspicious of or reacted negatively to direct marketing efforts, either due to over-inflated offers for products that did not live up to their promise or the complete lack of fulfillment by illegitimate businesses. Recent research has sought to investigate attitudes toward more modern direct marketing efforts, measuring attitudes toward unsolicited postal mail and e-mail. The results indicate that respondents viewed spam more annoying than direct mail solicitations sent through regular mail (Moromoto & Chang, 2006). Other research has focused on consumers' concerns about the privacy of the information they are sharing with direct marketers (Dolnicar & Jordaan, 2007)

Despite the attitudes toward some forms of direct marketing, consumers and companies alike realize a number of different benefits from this form of promotion. For consumers, direct marketing offers convenience and privacy. Simply by examining a catalog or website, consumers have at their fingertips a multitude of products they can compare and evaluate. Though they cannot physically touch the products, they can save enormous time that would be spent driving from store to store. Further, with today's sophisticated shipping options, consumers can receive their products quickly and conveniently at their home or office. For companies using this promotional tool, direct marketing helps streamline the distribution channel and logistics functions, resulting in a more cost-effective, efficient operation (Armstrong & Kotler, 2013). Websites, for example, afford companies greater flexibility and control over pricing offers or product descriptions. Finally, the global nature of the Internet lets companies expand their reach beyond the range that could be served with a physical store location.

The variety of options through which companies can execute their direct marketing efforts are another advantage, for both the company and the consumer, offering flexibility and choice where Sellers and Buyers can come together to execute the value exchange. These options are reviewed in Table 7.4.

As can be seen from the review of the tools in the Promotion Mix, marketers have a variety of communication options they can use to implement their marketing strategy. It should be noted, that not all of the tools are used for every marketing strategy. Each of the Promotional tools has its strengths and weaknesses and should be used thoughtfully—in a manner that will best facilitate the value exchange. In the next section, we will review the application of these promotional tools to an educational setting.

Promotion for the Educational Marketplace

Promotional activities are not new for schools, but in many cases schools have historically only utilized the public relation components of the promotional mix, with a heavy focus on communications. Given their cost effectiveness and the previous public climate that was found to be far more supportive of educational efforts, good public relations and communications was, arguably, all schools really needed to consider. As schools have become more embroiled in political conversations, community re-development efforts, and legislative reform efforts, promotion of your school is no longer about rallying a big crowd for Friday night's game. In order to truly maximize the promotional piece of the marketing mix, it is important to know how to effectively utilize each promotional tool for an educational context.

TABLE 7.4—Direct Marketing Options

Catalog marketing	Direct marketing efforts that include print, video, or digital catalogs that are mailed to select customers.
Direct mail marketing	Attempts to promote offers to customers by sending announcements, or other solicitations directly to individuals via the postal service.
Direct-response television marketing	An approach to the television advertising message that includes a method of response such as an address, telephone number, or website whereby members of the audience can respond directly to the advertiser in order to purchase a product or service offered in the advertising message. This can include short commercials, paid-programming, or collaborations with direct response television networks.
Face-to-face direct marketing	Utilizing a personal selling network to directly market products to consumers. This is sometimes called network marketing.
Kiosk marketing	Using self-service ordering machines stationed in convenient, high-traffic locations to market products directly to consumers. This is sometimes called automatic vending.
Online marketing	Efforts to market products and services over the Internet through websites, online ads, search engine marketing, and other web-based promotional outlets.
Telemarketing	Marketing to customers through use of the telephone, which can include both inbound and outbound selling efforts.

(AMA, 2013; Armstrong & Kotler, 2013)

Advertising is expensive. It is expensive because it has the most potential to reach the largest audience. If a school has a "big picture" idea, new program, or new mission that it wants everyone to know, advertising may be the way to go. If the cost of the advertising is out-weighted by the larger potential impact on the school, a purposeful and strategic media plan should be developed. The media plan should include:

Plan Objective: What is your ultimate goal for this advertising campaign? What do you want everyone to walk away from your advertisement understanding, feeling, doing?

Target Audience: Who is your target audience? What are their media habits? Which media forms and outlets do they utilize?

Messaging Strategy: How can schools align their plan objective with a message that the target audience will embrace? What images do you want the audience to have of the school or advertising campaign objective?

Timeline: What is the timeline for your end goal of the advertising campaign? Does the audience have enough time to respond to your advertisement? When do you want your message to be fresh in your audience's mind? How long can you afford to run the campaign?

Budget: How much will this advertising campaign cost? Does the school need to hire consultants, videographers, photographers, writers, or advertising agencies? What funds can you use to pay for the campaign? Does the potential benefits of the campaign match the fiscal realities of the school?

Assessment: Did your school meet the media plan objective? Did your school reach your target audience? Did your campaign leave the desired impression of your school on your audience? Did your messaging have the desired effect? Did you achieve your timeline? Did you stay within your budget and garner the potential benefits?

Following this basic framework for establishing an advertising campaign could be a very valuable promotional tool for schools, especially big schools with lots of stakeholders. In some cases it may be the only tool needed. In others, it may be one piece of a more dynamic mix of promotional tools. Public relation efforts allow you to tailor your message based on varying groups of stakeholders. Given that it is one of the more cost effective ways of promoting, it is understandably one of the most utilized tools by schools. There are several facets of public relations that may be incorporated into your overall promotional activities. These could include:

Media Relations: For most schools this happens in the form of press releases, television interviews, newspaper articles, as well as scripted public comments.

Product Publicity: Does your community see the value in what your school offers or the role your school plays in the community? When people in the community talk about your school, what do they say? When you do an Internet search of your school, what pops up? How is your school portrayed in the media, excluding paid advertisements?

Lobbying: Many schools are becoming more engaged with the political process. According to Fowler (2004), *The current reform movement can be seen as a revolt against the aging school organization inherited from the nineteenth and early twentieth centuries and as a search for a new paradigm . . . For the foreseeable future, the education policy scene will be turbulent with many new policy proposals, many changes, and many failed experiments . . . When systems are in flux, individuals have a chance to exercise influence that they do not have when systems are stable. Thus, those school leaders who want to, will be able to identify those trends in their states or districts that they support and work to advance them (p. 348).* As federal and local budgets get tighter, understanding the tenor and climate of state and federal educational policies becomes increasingly more necessary. A public school needs specific expertise in getting bonds and bond referendums on the ballot, in addition to having a voice in education reform efforts at the local, state, and federal levels. Many of the professional organizations in the field of education now have active advocacy groups.

Investor Relations: Stakeholders that make a fiscal contribution or significant impact on your school would be included in this group. Donors, alumni, families, and in some cases, taxpayers and private corporations could all be considered investors. Schools need to engage with these groups to garner support for endowments, capitol campaigns, or special events and scholarships.

Development and Maintenance of Positive Relations with Stakeholders: Generating awareness about your school is the cornerstone of this promotional activity. It is important to raise the interest of community stakeholders in your school and the services it provides. In many ways, what has previously been known as family engagement has begun to look more like customer service.

Personal selling is the piece of the promotional mix that can be important in addressing recruitment and retention issues. Personal selling is divided into two segments, inside sales and outside sales. Gauging the experiences of your students, staff, and families with your school would be considered inside sales activities that support student retention. Outside sales would consist of your school's activities focused on the recruitment of new students, staff, and families. The importance of both recruitment and retention, as well as building a focused personal selling plan, cannot be over emphasized.

Special events, presentations, and booths at conventions, vouchers, and sample classes could all be considered educational versions of sales promotions. Some schools offer scholarships toward tuition and housing. Other schools offer free remediation, discounts on technology and clothing, or child care services for an introductory time period. Attending extracurricular events at a reduced price or touring classes and campuses could also be considered sales promotion. Direct marketing is the most focused piece of the promotional mix.

When you have a specific message for a specific audience in a specific time frame, direct marketing is a good option. Many schools now utilize technology and social media to spread the word. School websites and social media outlets can be used to convey a message effectively and timely; to share news about a weather delay for example. For others, automatic telephone calls conveying information to stakeholders has been found effective. Many teachers utilize social media as a way to update families on class activities and provide homework support, while coaches may use it to update community members about the school's performance at out-of-state competitions.

Promotional activities require a considerable amount of resources, but when used effectively, can yield much greater returns. With so many options in the promotional mix, aligning efforts across and within your educational institution will be crucial. The next section offers recommendations for coordinating promotional efforts across buildings and programs.

Coordinating District Level and Building Level Efforts

Though most of the leadership of marketing efforts in schools, be it public or private, will come from either a director of communication, or an administrator who works in the central office, it is very important to remember the vast majority of the contacts needed for support are personal, one-on-one interactions. Political campaigns know this and that is why they develop a broad overarching

Cameron Whitman/Shutterstock.com

message that will be played out in television, print, and Internet advertisements, but they also recruit and depend upon volunteers (some who are paid) to go door-to-door and make the local contacts. It is well known that the local contacts are often the big difference between winning and losing elections. Canvassing and supporting those who canvass is vital to success. The canvassers may be saying nothing different from the candidates themselves (may be even the same, culled from a provided script), but it is the local contact and hearing from others that build support and momentum.

Remembering the importance of canvassers for political candidates is very important for schools as they develop a message. It is not so much that school district employees are expected to go door-to-door, but that others may have developed a message and the teachers (playing a similar role as the canvassers) help spread the message and be the point of contact for everyone else. Typically the person or group who develops the message cannot meet with everyone who will be impacted by the intent of the message, be it helping to recruit new students or to get a new bond measure passed. It is vital that others help spread the message and that the information being disseminated is easy enough for others to digest, but it is also easy for others to help spread.

This is why there needs to be clear communication and coordination between the district and building level efforts. There is more below, on working together as a team; this is a process that is far too often ignored. Much like when businesses develop a new product but have not trained the staff on the details, schools need to keep the frontline personnel very aware of the steps, strategies, and needs, of any marketing plans. The following are some quick steps that should be employed in conveying information to building level personnel:

1. Place a member of the building level staff on the team developing the plan. They know the in's and out's of the day-to-day responsibilities of the building level employees. They can talk about the time involved, and they can discuss the typical questions that would be asked from parents and from others in the community. Having a building level person on the committee can also shield complaints that the new plan is too "top-down" and did not involve others.

2. Develop a short summary of the plan. Explain the rationale behind the effort, provide some history, and explain what would happen if the plan is not put into place.

3. Develop as many frequently asked questions about the proposal as possible, with short, bullet style answers. This will make it easier for others to refer to and answer questions about in the future.

4. Hold an open forum where the above information is presented and any and all questions can be asked. Have the necessary people in the room who can answer the questions and address any concerns.

5. Make sure there is a person who will serve as a point of contact when there are questions. For example, if there is a question that a teacher or building level principal cannot address, make sure there is one person who can answer any and all questions in a timely fashion. It is important that this person realize if there are too many questions coming their way, that more and better information needs to be provided to the building level personnel.

Promotion in Education

Promotion seems easier in business than in education. Many businesses know that if they do not promote their product or the services they provide, they will not be in business anymore. It is not necessarily that the need for the business or the services will no longer be needed (though that is the case for manufacturers of VCR's and beepers), it is more likely that someone else will take over and do it instead. Public education has not seemed to have a need for promotion, with its captive audience and fairly fixed market share. But times have changed, and private, charter, and online schools are changing the landscape very dramatically.

Similar to the business world, prior to the Internet, the messages provided by education to the rest of the world was very one-sided, with the information coming from the schools and being delivered out to others. Schools were also known for one thing, and did not really have to cater to the many different needs of the students in their schools, and did not have to tell others about these efforts. Additionally, there was not a need for schools to have to think about consistent marketing efforts and message, everyone knew what they did and there was no question.

Promotion of school efforts has also been confused with advertising. Public schools have consistently had problems with promotion. Private and charter school have not. But public schools need to become more aware of the needs for promotion as their districts are being affected by bond and budget issues.

The following is an example of the coordinated efforts by a district and building to prevent extensive cuts by a new school board. The issue might not be the same as the ones you are dealing with, but the steps for conceptualizing the plan are appropriate and should be considered.

School Budget Under Attack

Very few candidates campaign on a desire to raise taxes for schools, but it seems that many campaign to cut taxes. While public school educators cannot actively campaign for or against different candidates as a representative of the school, they can actively help the public understand the role they play in society and the benefits of a public education.

In one particular election in Pennsylvania, it seemed like all the candidates running for school board had solely as their emphasis to cut taxes and slash spending for public schools. This occurred despite the fact that some of the schools were starting to get crowded. All projections for the next ten years indicated continued unsustainable growth. The middle schools and the high school had been updated relatively recently and looked like they would be able to handle the new students, though there might be crowded halls and lunchrooms. Clearly though, there was a very specific need to at least keep funding where it was because of the sheer volume of demands being placed on the schools.

A few of the candidates proposed extensive and severe cuts to the school budget. Some of the candidates announced their plans over a year in advance, giving time for the school leaders to plan. All indications, however, was that the public on the whole supported the schools. However, it was an off-year election and the school staff was concerned that only individuals VERY concerned about the local issues would show up to vote. There was a lot of energy on the cut taxes sides, but the school leaders were unsure how deep was their support.

The superintendent and the board decided it would be good to have one member of the administrative team, the assistant superintendent for finance, and three members of the board develop a task force to start the planning for educating the public about what the school does for the community. They developed a seven-point plan:

1. Leave no detail unchecked
2. Develop a simple message
3. Make sure this is a team effort
4. Build a great plan
5. Motivate the team
6. Take the long approach to groundwork
7. Develop six very clear statements

This plan was the basis for all efforts. It took time, some money, but a concerted effort to identify what needed to be done ahead of time. They viewed this as a two-year plan, ahead of the election. This allowed for greater planning, emphasis on details, and also to make sure they let the public know what they really did for the community.

Step One—Leave No Detail Unchecked

Make a list of every possible question someone could ask about the public schools. Questions they came up with included:

1. What are the enrollment projections for the next ten years?
2. What will be the enrollment of the new school?
3. How much is spent per pupil in this district versus other districts?
4. Where does the money come from?
5. How much does the state provide?
6. Does the school provide special transportation to students with disabilities?
7. How much money is spent on sports?
8. How much money is spent on computers?
9. How much does a teacher make?
10. How much does an aide make?
11. Where can we cut services?
12. How large are class sizes?
13. Is a new school necessary or can we just use portable classrooms?
14. Can we cut languages?
15. Can we cut band?
16. Can we cut sports?

People in the district want to see exactly what they're getting for their money. The credibility that you project with your knowledge and the people who are on board give the community great comfort that the district spends money wisely.

Step Two—Develop a Simple Message

Most people who will be voting do not have time to read through detailed reports about overcrowding and the problems associated with too many students in a classroom, or they do not understand what to look for in ten-year projections of student enrollment. Keep the main message simple. The message they chose was, "Don't forget to vote to support kids education on November 4." This was the message given to the parents at PTO meetings, hung on the billboards outside of town, and provided for the numerous bumper stickers one saw around town. On the district's webpage they developed a list of FAQ's to help get the information across for those who needed greater detail (see list of questions above).

They chose this very simple message because it reminded the voters of the affirmative obligation required to support schools, that of actively going to vote on Election Day. They also made sure the date of the election was also included because for this election cycle there was no other major (presidential or congressional) seat on the ballot, and few seemed to be paying attention to the election. They also chose this very simple message because it implied all you needed to do to support kids was to vote on this day, and that nothing else was required.

Step Three—Make Sure This Is a Team Effort

Money spent on public schools does not just affect the students and employees of the school, it affects the whole town. Therefore, they needed to highlight the benefits to others in the town and use them to help share the responsibility of convincing others that schools are necessary. Others they identified that are clearly affected include real estate agents, shopkeepers, the local chamber of commerce, builders, sports associations, and groups of ministers that are in their area. Good schools reverberate across a town in ways that most people forget and often don't realize. It can truly bring a town together—if done correctly. They realized the more community leaders they could get on their side, the easier it would be to get the message out. They spent a lot of time with representatives going to Rotary Club meetings, Kiwanis, and Chamber of Commerce breakfasts.

One thing they kept in mind when seeking support for public schools (or for any major change at the schools) is to not wait until their support is needed. They realized they needed prominent members of the school district's administration as members of community organizations, and provided speakers on topics even when they were not asking for their support. It is very good community building but also kept others informed about they were doing.

Step Four—Build a Great Plan

You need a new elementary school? You need to convince the voting public this is also needed. In this case, they just wanted to preserve the public schools. They developed a plan for convincing others of this. Meeting with leaders in the community, as mentioned above, was a very good way of doing this. But they also realized they need to talk with community leaders about any perceived problems they were having. How recent was the last time the district asked for a bond measure for a school? Is there a pervasive mood of unhappiness with the schools and an attitude the public schools are a waste of money? Or, is there such a sentiment against public spending, even though there might not be a tax increase?

Many of the above questions were addressed with discussions with leaders in the community. The last few required polling efforts to help determine the prevailing sentiment of the community at-large.

Step Five—Motivate the Team

They thought of their team as all the YES voters in the district—those supporting candidates for school board who didn't want to slash the school budget. They willingly went to any and all forums they could go to, and also willingly answered all questions from all candidates. It was very clear, however, that the only candidates requesting information from the district were candidates who were interested in not drastically cutting the budget. Also, though the district made all candidates aware they could send a representative to a forum, again, only candidates not interested in massive cuts to the budget took them up on this offer.

The job was to get the YES voters to the polls on the right date. There will always be voters in the district who can be referred to as CAVE (can't accept virtually everything) voters. These voters, no matter how much one does, likely would never support public money being spent for schools, and educators need to realize this and not take it personally. The job is not to convince everyone in the district to support schools, only enough YES voters on the right date. It is helpful to try and identify the YES voters, but also the leaning votes—those who would probably vote yes and support the cause.

Step Six—Take the Long Approach to Groundwork

The district realized they may have priorities, but those priorities may not be the same as what the electorate is willing to pay for. As noted above, they ran some polling to try and determine what the public was willing to support and what the public is absolutely refusing to support. For example, the football stadium may be crumbling and the support for a new stadium is very vocal, but not very deep, is an indication of something that the public would be often unlikely to support. Determine early on what is needed, and also what would be supported.

Step Seven—Develop Six Very Clear Statements

They developed a plan where they would come up with quick statements they would say about the school. The ability to intertwine good comments about an institution that has taken a beating in public opinion is very important. If they were not going to say good things about the school who was? Most people only hear negative comments about schools, especially when there is violence or low-test scores, they never hear about the good things schools do, or have done.

They worked with the administrative team to develop statements emphasizing the good things the public would understand about the schools. They all have to be one sentence long, and not filled with educational jargon. They came up with a list of statements that you could use when talking with anyone's grandmother at the local Labor Day picnic. They never had to use more than two or three, but they were ready when someone made a negative statement about public schools. They found it was also important to try and figure how to incorporate them into normal everyday conversation, instead of just walking up to someone and start spouting.

Statement examples:

1. We provide a comprehensive reading, math, music, and arts program for all our students.
2. Over 85% of our students graduate from school.
3. Over 65% of our students go on to higher education.
4. 65% of our teachers hold masters degrees or higher.
5. Many of our teachers have become experts in their field and have taught over ten years.
6. We have a new program to attract young talented teachers to our schools.
7. We have one of the best sets of test scores of any schools in our area.
8. We have over 100 applicants for each teaching job. We only take the best.
9. Our school debate team is one of the best in the state.
10. Our (pick a sport) sports team is one of the best in the state.
11. Our district made Annual Yearly Progress last year. We are very proud of that.
12. We offer more electives at our high school than most schools.
13. Our students get into the colleges they want to go to.
14. We have a security plan that is very good and the teachers are continually trained for emergencies.

The League of Women Voters sponsored a debate. All candidates came. It became very clear the only candidates aware of what was going on in the schools were the candidates who had talked with school officials about the need for certain subjects and certain expenditures. The audience was filled with teachers and school administrators. The candidates who wanted to slash the school budget could not come up with specifics to cut, other than "fat" or "waste." The other candidates, however, spoke eloquently about the need for, and continued support of, current and continued expenditures for public education.

Aftermath—the candidates supporting maintaining the current school budget all won handily. The schools felt like they received a boost from their support. The district realized the need for continued awareness for the community about what they do and decided to not stop and wait for the next election, but to make sure they worked to get the message out about what they do.

Conclusion

Promotion is difficult for some schools to understand. However, it is a vital part of the process for schools to get their message out to others. Doing a really good job at the day-to-day responsibilities is the most important part of what we do in education. However, in order for us to continue to do what we want and need to do, we need to make sure others are aware of the successes. This is a very important shift for many educators to realize. Without this shift, what you do and how your school goes about providing services might go away.

Chapter Seven—Spotlight: Community Prep School

Just sit back and think, what if tomorrow started thirty-eight consecutive days of negative stories about your school in the press? Is your stomach starting to turn? Let's add to the equation that you get no warning or time to prepare and the Associated Press will carry your story in several well-known European news outlets. Are you beginning to feel queasier? Well, for the staff at Community Prep School (CPS) that became a reality.

CPS is an urban K–12 charter school. Sixteen percent of CPS students have an IEP and another 30% qualify for English as a new language services. Ninety three percent of CPS students qualify for free and reduced lunch and during the previous school year, 84% of CPS students passed the state standardized test. After operating quietly for several years, with top academic performance and admirable community engagement, CPS was suddenly thrust into the middle of a heated political scandal. While neither the school, nor its staff or students, had done anything wrong, they still got thrown around in the public media like a rag doll. If the coverage had been about test scores or a situation with a student they would have been prepared. There were communication plans in place for typical educational issues; but being so far removed and having so little information about the actual political scandal they were being associated with was completely unexpected and foreign to the staff at CPS.

The toll on staff and students was great. Teachers and students alike were being called names by the staff and students at other schools. They were made to feel their years of hard work and accomplishments had been compromised. In some cases, teachers felt exceptionally uncomfortable with comments and questions from their own children's teachers. Students and teachers were harassed via social media and the school had to establish a security plan to ensure the press was not just walking through the front door unannounced.

The CPS school leader was facing what most educators would consider a professional nightmare. How do you protect your students and staff? How do you protect your reputation and ability to recruit future students? The stakes could not be higher. CPS took a two-pronged approach. First they handled internal issues and took care of their school community:

1. Contact IT and get your facts straight. They went through all communications and e-mails related to the topic back ten years to ensure they had all the information correct. They then followed up and checked with staff to make sure their information was correct.
2. Day Two Staff Meeting. They shared this information with their staff, students, and families first. They wanted them to have all of the correct information and have time and space to ask questions and get more comfortable with their approach to this problem.
3. Protect the school day. They made sure that students, staff, and families felt good about what they had done and coming to school. They assured them we would keep them safe from further intrusion.
4. Provide support. The CPS leadership team made themselves and counseling services available for students, families, and staff that needed additional support.

At the same time, the school created a plan for handling external issues as well:

1. Be thoughtful and strategic! At the time it feels urgent, your instincts tell you to respond quickly and get ahead of it. It is not a good idea to respond in the moment. If it is thrust upon you, it is impossible to get ahead of. The decisions and actions you make in the early stages of this process are critical.
2. Get the facts straight. Make sure you have your facts correct and have notified everyone internally about your process. Release a statement based on facts and your position on the topic.
3. Only grant interviews to press with established ground rules. Deny all requests for interviews and only speak on the record with press that you have invited in to do interviews. Make sure you outline what you will discuss and what you won't, as well as asking to see articles and pieces prior to publication. This may not be granted, but conveying the question in initial negotiations is important. In many ways this is your story; you may not control the initial incident but you can control your response.
4. Create a central theme and be consistent. CPS was able to tailor their actual communication with the community, stakeholders, employees, and others, while sticking to the same script.
5. Hire help. CPS hired a lawyer and public relations consultant on temporary contracts to help navigate the uncharted waters.

Questions

1. What was one thing that CPS did that you can implement in a crisis communication plan?
2. How can your messaging be tailored to different groups of stakeholders with a central theme or unplanned events? Provide an example.
3. Discuss a time when you had to navigate the media. How did your strategy compare to CPS's strategy?

Applying the Concepts

1. How do you think this experience with the media impacted CPS's budget? What would this mean for your own advertising and budgeting?
2. How does your use of social media, newsletters, newspapers, television, and telephone calling inform each other? Are they aligned, redundant, or conflicting? Do you have social media policies in place?
3. Do you know which stakeholders are utilizing which modes of communication? Why is this important?

References

Armstrong, G., & Kotler, P. (2013). *Marketing: An Introduction* (11th ed.). Boston, MA: Pearson.

Baack, D. (1997). *Organizational Behavior*. Houston, TX: Dame Publications.

Buiness Wire. Research Reveals Word-of-Mouth Campaigns on Customer Networks Double Marketing Results. (27 October). Retrieved March 5, 2010, from ABI/INFORM Dateline. (Document ID: 1887268081).

Calder, B. (2008). *Kellogg on Advertising and Media*. Hoboken, NJ: John Wiley & Sons.

Clow, K., & Baack, D. (2001). *Integrated Advertising, Promotion and Marketing Communications*. Upper Saddle River, NJ: Prentice Hall.

DMA. (2011). *The DMA 2011 Statistical Fact Book*, 33rd ed. February, 2011.

Dolnicar, S., & Jordaan, Y. (2007). A market-oriented approach to responsibly managing information privacy concerns in direct marketing. *Journal of Advertising, 35*(2), 123–149.

Fowler, F. C. (2004). *Policy studies for educational leaders: An introduction*. Upper Saddle River, NJ: Pearson.

Kotler, P., & Keller, K. (2012). *Marketing Management* (14th ed.). Boston, MA: Prentice Hall.

Moromoto, M., & Chang, S. (2006). Consumers' attitudes toward unsolicited commercial e-mail and postal direct mail marketing methods: Intrusiveness, perceived loss of control, and irritation. *Journal of Interactive Advertising, 7*(1), 8–20.

PRSA. (2013). Terms of use. Retrieved from http://www.prsa.org/AboutPRSA/PublicRelationsDefined/

Chapter 8

Pulling It All Together

In the end, all business operations can be reduced to three words: people, product, and profits. Unless you've got a good team, you can't do much with the other two.

—*Lee Iacocca*, Former President, CEO and Chairman of the Chrysler Corporation

As we have advocated throughout, a solid understanding of the marketing mix is necessary before any promotion activities or integrated marketing communication can be executed. Building any marketing campaign begins with understanding the needs and wants of the target audience and assembling an entire marketing mix of product, price, place, and promotion that will motivate consumers to engage in the value exchange. Some organizations waste time and resources creating products and services, with no regard for consumers' needs or whether the product would be desired. They then attempt to "market" the product through a series of tired communication methods that do not reach the intended audience and, when all of this fails, they throw even more money trying to push a product that customers didn't want in the first place. Leaving marketing communication to pick up the slack of a poorly conceived product concept is like using a coat of paint to cover up cracks in the wall. It won't take care of the problem.

Once a marketing plan has been put together, implementation can begin. However, implementing marketing communication activities to support the overall marketing plan can take considerable forethought, coordination and—sometimes—delegation. Often, inexperienced marketers do not allow enough lead time to execute the promotional effort. Say, for example, an elementary school is hosting an admissions open house during the first weekend of November and seeks to utilize a number of communications outlets, each of which has a different lead time, in terms of production. This kind of event entails the involvement of many different parties—such as outside vendors, staff, and other members of the school community. The calendar following shows how far out planning for the event must begin.

TABLE 8.1—Sample Marketing Calendar for School Open House

Date	Action	Responsible Party/Supplier	Comments
4–5 weeks prior	Mailer	School sends out direct mail postcard announcing the event.	Up to a month before the postcard is mailed, work with printer/mail house to design, print, purchase mailing list (or use existing database list, if applicable), etc.
3 weeks prior	Yard signs	Utilize Parent Association to help distribute signs and get them into yards surrounding school.	Signs must be designed and sent to printer up to a month prior to distribution date.
2 weeks prior	E-mail blasts	Generated by school	Sent to entire school community, urging them to come, spread the word, etc. Repeat 1 week out.
2 weeks prior	Media Release	Generated by school	Sent to local media outlets. Ex: Radio PSA (public service announcement), newspaper release, etc.
November 1	Open House	Hosted by School	Food, decorations, brochures, faculty staff on hand to welcome guests.
1 week after	Yard sign collection	Utilize Parent Association to help get the signs down and returned to school.	Find out from printer whether they can be stored and re-used (simply by updating the date information).
1–2 weeks after	Admissions follow up	Admissions staff	Follow up with interested families on questions. Ask them in for a shadow day, etc.
1–2 weeks after	Staff de-briefing	Faculty/Staff/Parent Assn.	Get feedback from faculty and staff on what worked, how the event could be improved upon.
1–2 weeks after	Measurement/ analysis	Admissions staff	Analyze metrics tied to goal: Ex: attendance counts, comments from attendees, requests for information, shadow dates set, enrollments, etc. In addition, examine effectiveness of marketing communication activities by asking attendees how they learned about the open house. Track effectiveness of each promotional tool to measure effectiveness of each. Save measurement data for future benchmarking/comparisons.

As the calendar in Table 8.1 demonstrates, marketers are continually challenged to think and plan well ahead of an actual event. In addition, the table shows that, from initial implementation to final measurement, the school can devote nearly two months of activity to the successful execution of a single marketing-related activity. The measurement and follow-up activities that occur after a marketing event are critical to the ongoing success of any marketing organization; unfortunately, many organizations skip this step. However, analyzing the response to the marketing goals are the only way an organization can truly determine if the implementation of the plan was a success or not.

Evaluating the Return on Your Marketing Investment

At first, many organizations look only at the bottom line when determining whether or not a marketing program was a success. They calculate the net profits derived from a marketing effort divided by the funds spent to generate that profit. However, as we have discussed throughout, not every marketing goal relates to sales or profits. Furthermore, it is not always possible to attribute a customer's action or response to a particular marketing activity. For example, a young couple, with no children, may purchase a home in a district. They live and work in the area and may have limited knowledge of the local schools. Perhaps they read in the paper about some award the high school band won or see on the news that a teacher from one of the elementary schools has been recognized with a teaching award. A few years later, they read about the Superintendent's plan for updating the computer labs at all of the middle schools or perhaps they see a billboard celebrating the scholarships and achievements of the high school graduating class. All of these communication touch points begin to build an impression on the couple. Later, when their own children are toddlers, they receive an information pamphlet in the mail from the local school on the topic of school-readiness and school-selection for parents of pre-school children. A year later, they notice yard signs promoting a school open house event and they decide to attend. Two months later, they register their oldest child for kindergarten at the nearby elementary school. Which of these marketing-related activities should receive credit for the ultimate enrollment of the child? The media relations activities? The fact that the school has award-winning teachers? The investment in updated computers? The brochure? The open house? The ultimate decision is most likely rooted in all of these—which is why marketing is difficult to measure. No single measure is likely to be perfect, which is why more sophisticated marketers use a "portfolio or dashboard" of metrics (Farris, Bendle, Pfiefer, & Reibstein, 2006).

The appropriate metric to use in measuring marketing performance should be tied to the specific goal. To begin, there are tools which can be used to quantify the response to a marketing effort. These can include attendance figures, total sales, number of gross impressions generated by an ad campaign, and even the number of page-views of a website. There are also metrics which can be used to measure the operational performance of marketing efforts, such as profitability analysis, rates of return, and customer profitability. Finally, there are measurements which can be taken to evaluate intangible variables, like attitudes, loyalty, or recall. Based on the results of the evaluation techniques used, the appropriate changes or improvements can be implemented in the planning and implementation of future open house events. This last point illuminates the fact that marketing is a cyclical process, from planning to implementation, to evaluation and back to planning.

The key effective evaluation is to select the metrics that provide the best insights into how the marketing efforts achieved the established goal—and what adjustments need to be made moving forward. However, it should also be noted that sometimes the performance measurement can help an organization realize that the goal itself was unrealistic. For example, after they had established a new database for tracking blood donors, a local blood center established a goal to increase the number of returning donors of a particular blood-type by 50%. This was not a statistic the center had ever attempted to track before and they had no idea what kind of response they would receive to their new plans to promote on-going donations. After implementing a targeted communications program aimed at donors of the critical blood-type, the center measured a 23% increase in repeat visits by the desired donors. They were amazed at the positive response to their new strategy and how well they were able to meet the demand for particular blood types. Nonetheless, a 23% response rate

Monkey Business Images/Shutterstock.com

was less than half of their stated goal. They concluded that their efforts were, in fact, successful and were helping to improve the efficient performance of the center. However, they also determined that they had set an unrealistic goal—which is understandable, given the fact that they were attempting something completely new.

Continuing with the open house example discussed earlier in this chapter, the chart below lists the activities and how they might be evaluated.

TABLE 8.2—School Open House Evaluation Metrics

Action	Goal	Possible Evaluation Metric
Mailer	Send out 1,000 postcards to promote event.	Track returned address cards to update database.
Yard signs	Utilize Parent Association to help distribute signs and get them into yards surrounding school.	Track number of signs sent out, and number of signs returned for potential future use.
E-mail blasts	Send 5,000 e-mail messages to entire database asking them to help spread the word about the event.	Track e-mail bounce-backs and use information to clean up the database.
Media Release	Send to all radio, TV, newspaper, etc., with goal of having them all announce the event.	Track number of media outlets who ran the announcement. If newspaper, for example, use circulation figures to track gross impressions.
Open House	250 new families attend.	Use a sign-in card to collect information about the attendees. Count total number of families. Track any additional information, such as how they heard about the event (mailer, yard sign, etc.)
Admissions follow-up	Of the families who attend, get 1/3 to commit to schedule a shadow visit.	Track number of shadow visits scheduled from open house attendees.

Other metrics which could be used to evaluate the success of the plan include basic financial calculations to gauge the level of spending against the level of return. For example, the school could tally the costs associated with printing postcards and yard signs, along with all of the other costs associated with the event, such as decorations, food, and the like to measure the return on the marketing investment. Based on the results of the evaluation techniques used, the appropriate changes or improvements can be implemented in the planning and implementation of future open house events.

Once a school begins to get a sense of measuring response rates to individual activities, they can then move to examining the overall expenditures it takes to generate the kind of response they are seeking, For example, by tracking the costs associated with every admission-related activity, the school could then begin to get a picture of the marketing-related expenditures required to generate an enrollment in the school, a metric similar to what businesses refer to as average acquisition costs, which can be calculated using the formula below.

FIGURE 8.1—Average Acquisition Cost

$$\frac{\text{Acquisition Spending (\$)}}{\text{Number of Customers Acquired (\#)}}$$

Likewise, schools could track the marketing-related expenses they incur to keep students in the school—such as community-night events—to track their retention costs, which can be calculated using the formula below.

FIGURE 8.2—Average Retention Cost

$$\frac{\text{Retention Spending (\$)}}{\text{Number of Customers Retained (\#)}}$$

By comparing the two figures, the school can get a sense of what it spends to generate a new enrollment, relative to what it takes to retain a student. These kind of additional metrics allow a school to make a better connection between the limited funds available for marketing projects and the impact they have on the school and its bottom line.

Other metrics which may prove useful to a school are listed in the table below.

TABLE 8.3—Marketing Metrics for Schools

Metric	How toApply	Purpose
Market Share	Total students of a school divided by the total number of available students in a market.	Shows where a school stands relative to all of its competition.
Marketing Spending	Add total fixed marketing costs (such as labor, long-term advertising commitments or admissions/promotional material) with total variable marketing costs, such as those tied to particular events or marketing communication.	Allows a school to analyze where money on marketing is being spent, relative to the school's operating budget.
Retention Rate	The ratio of students retained to students lost.	Tracks the school's ability to retain students.
Impressions	The count of the number of times an ad is viewed.	This enables the school to track the reach of its advertising.
Average Frequency	Counts the average number of times an individual is exposed to an ad.	Advertising needs to be repeated to make an impact on an audience. Some advertising mediums (such as billboards) are more cost effective at delivering repeated exposure than others.
Page Views	The number of times a web page is seen.	Web analytics provide considerable insights into where people are looking at your website, how they found your site, how much time they are spending on your sight, etc. Analytic trackers (such as Google analytics) are easy to add to your site's operation.
Cost per Click	In search engine advertising, the amount spent divided by the number of clicks the ad received.	Search engine advertising (such as Google AdWords) can be a cost effective way to reach an audience who may be using search terms to look for a specialized program.

Utilizing marketing metrics allows schools to develop a more cost-effective and strategic view of how marketing activities contribute to the school's overall operation. Likewise, it enables schools to make comparisons between activities that produce the desired results and those that don't—relative to the dollars spent to produce the result. Metrics help take the guesswork, emotion, and tradition out of the marketing planning process.

Using Social Media

Many organizations have used social media to help engage their customers in ways they never could before. Recognizing that students are heavily involved in social media, many schools are eager to add this platform to their marketing communications regimen. However, schools should be cautioned to educate themselves about social media before diving in blindly. According to the 2013 Social Media Marketing Industry Report, 86% of marketing professionals believe that social media is important to their business; however nearly 90% of them want to know which tactics are the most effective at engaging their audience (Stelzner, 2013). Social media encompasses a variety of communications vehicles. They include blogs, podcasts, social media sites such as Facebook, Twitter, Instagram, Pinterest, etc., as well as YouTube. However, beyond simply maintaining a blog or a Facebook page, marketers must understand how to measure the effectiveness of their social media activities.

For schools, there are pro's and con's to using social media. Without going into an exhaustive list, we shall consider some of the factors that are important to schools. First, social media is free to use. Where billboards and radio ads cost money, social media is free. Depending on how it is managed, social media can reach a large audience and it can also reach a targeted one. On the downside, social media is extremely time-consuming. Content has to be generated and maintained on a timely basis, or the organization will risk losing its connection with the audience—which is one of the primary reasons for utilizing social media marketing in the first place. Where traditional media involves sending out messages to an audience, social media marketing involves multi-directional communication—where users can initiate a topic, share, and respond to other messages with the organization or with each other. This represents a loss of control for the organization. Further, the targets for social media platforms are becoming ever-more fragmented. For example, Facebook used to be extremely popular

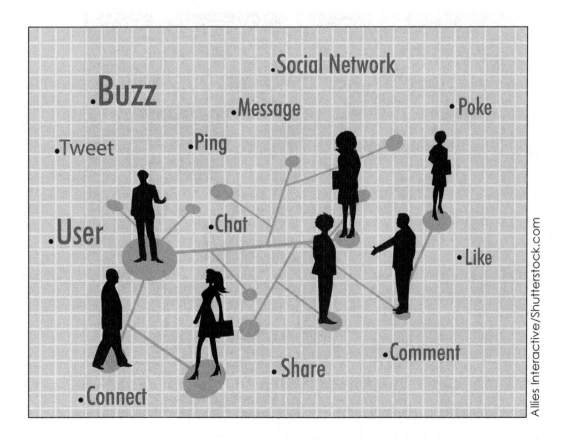

among teens—at least until their parents showed up on the site. As a result, teens moved to Instagram, Vine, Tumblr, and Snapchat. The ever-evolving use of social media sites helps marketers realize the importance of understanding why and how they want to use social media—and, most importantly—who they want to reach. Most schools focus on reaching parents, rather than students. Nonetheless, with limited human capital to devote toward managing social media messaging, schools are advised to tread lightly until they can develop a sustainable plan of action where social media marketing is concerned. To develop a social media plan, Chad Norman, from the nonprofit consulting firm Blackbaud, encourages nonprofits to answer a series of questions by using the "P.O.S.T. method" (Norman, 2009).

People	Who are you trying to engage?
Objectives	What are you trying to achieve?
Strategies	What will it look like when you are done?
Technologies	What are the tools you plan to use?

In developing a social media marketing strategy, there are five key components that should be addressed; these include: listening, planning, execution, monitoring, and measurement (Chapman, 2012). Once an organization has identified the audience they wish to attract, they must listen to find out where and how the audience wants to engage online. The planning calls for an evaluation of each social media platform, in terms of the reach and any other technical considerations. From there, a communication plan should be developed for each social channel, recognizing the differences that exist within each social network community. For example, Pinterest is extremely different from Facebook and organizations cannot simply copy and paste a single message across all platforms. With

Dusit/Shutterstock.com

respect to monitoring, the organization must have established, up-front goals against which they can measure the results. Goals can include simple counts, such as website visits, or complex analyses of the content generated in social media conversations.

In terms of technologies, schools are advised to be aware of how social media, blogs, or e-mail can be useful in driving traffic to a website, where more information can be provided, where people can sign up for events, or request more information. However, these actions will happen only if the digital experience is easy and pleasant for the user. With this in mind, schools are urged to evaluate their website to make sure it is user-friendly, accurate, and contains up-to-date information. For example, if a school wishes to use the website as an admissions tool, the site should include information parents will find useful in making a school-choice decision. This could include very detailed information about how to enroll a child in the school, such as FAQ's, key dates, necessary forms, or broader information which will help parents in their decision process, such as white papers or links to other sites.

At all times, however, schools cannot forget their position in the community and because social media involves other parties engaging in the communication, platforms must be monitored for appropriateness. With this in mind, it is useful for schools to have some sense of established policies for social media conduct. Likewise, schools should establish an oversight committee charged with monitoring and managing the school's social media governance. Such an audit should cover the following key questions (Whalen and Krishna, 2013):

1. Does the school's leadership understand how social media is affecting the organization?
    In other words, does the school fully appreciate the associated risks, in terms of the impact on the school's varied stakeholder groups?

2. Is someone monitoring the school's social media platforms to identify potential problems or opportunities?
    Does the school utilize a social media monitoring tool? There are several free tools, such as Hootsuite, TweetReach, Klout, Social Mention, Twazzup, Addictomatic, HowSociable, and IceRocket (Mindruta, 2013). This process should be incorporated into the organization's risk management process and the school should discuss how and when to respond to various issues being raised in social media conversations.

3. Does the school have a single, clearly defined policy regarding employee use of social media—both personal and professional, and on personal and professional devices?
    Teachers and coaches are popular members of a school community and their tweets or blogs could serve as important components of a social media strategy. However, the school should retain the right to monitor that content. Further, the school has a responsibility to properly train employees in the appropriate use of social media.

4. Does the school's social media governance structure provide enough guidance as to how the school community will be represented?
    The school should have formal guidelines for all contributors to social media so that they properly represent the school's brand message.

5. How will the school monitor compliance with the school's social media governance?
    This should also address enforcement. As public entities, schools are accountable to boards or charter-sponsors. As such, the school should be able to report its compliance to established social media policies and how it has handled itself in this public forum.

The preceding is not intended to scare schools from engaging in social media strategies. Rather, this information is provided to protect schools before problems arise. There are a number of useful resources for schools looking to establish the appropriate policies; for example, the website Social Media Governance (socialmediagovernance.com, 2013) provides a number of general guidelines and templates schools can adapt for their own use. A variety of resources cover blogging, social media, Internet, and e-mail policies and other best practices. As stated previously, schools should make sure their legal counsel or risk management office is involved in the development and oversight of a social media strategy.

Adopting a Marketing Orientation

As a result of increased competition, most school administrators realize that they respond to the challenges of the operating environment in which they now operate. Many have expressed the desire to "do more marketing." In most cases, "doing marketing" translates into putting out press releases or running ads in the local paper. While such communication efforts are often the visible end result of a carefully-planned marketing strategy, they do not, alone, represent an organization's marketing orientation. As we have advocated, marketing is an operational philosophy. The full marketing mix of product, price, place and—finally—promotion—work together to create the value proposition that meets a consumer's needs. Many nonmarketers look for a quick fix or they want a single checklist or playbook to follow, in order to show "marketing activity." Sadly, there is no single checklist that covers all marketing objectives and the simple reason is that consumers have different needs. There cannot be a single checklist because products, prices, places, and promotions all vary. The same holds true for schools. An organization that has truly adopted a marketing orientation focuses on customers and produces what they want. The truth is—that while the coordination and communication activities may reside within a marketing or communications function—marketing is an enterprise-wide undertaking that transcends ads, websites, and public relations.

Create a marketing-oriented organization "requires the widespread adoption of an organizational culture based on common values and a shared understanding of the market, as well as the distribution of intra-organizational power" (Gebhardt, Carpenter, & Sherry, 2009). Research into how organizations successfully adopt a market orientation reveals there are four distinct phases: (1) initiation, (2) reconstitution, (3) institutionalization, and (4) maintenance (Gebhardt, Carpenter, & Sherry, 2006).

Initiation—This phase encompasses two steps: recognition and preparation. The initiation stage begins when members of an organization recognize a threat. As a result, they mobilize to effect change. In the preparation step, a new leader emerges. In some cases, the leader is the individual who recognized the need for change; in other instances, organizational stakeholders who desire change appoint a new leader. Activities in the preparation step center around building a coalition of individuals or groups who share common values and have a similar vision for change. Lack of shared values or agreement on the direction to take to enact change have been found to be critical factors which can undermine an organization's ability to adopt a market orientation.

Reconstitution—This phases includes five distinct steps: demarcation, value, and norm development, reconnection with the market, removal of dissenters and hiring of believers, and adoption of a collaborative strategy. The demarcation step occurs when the leadership coalition presents its plan to the organization. Successful demarcation events include transparency, open to all members of the organization. In addition, the threat faced by the firm has to be explained as compellingly authentic. Perhaps most importantly, the process for change must be "framed as market focused, not marketing centric" (Gebhardt et al., 2006, p. 42.) In other words, it must be clear to the members of the entire organization that meeting customers' needs are driving the force behind the proposed change. Where formerly the organizational culture was quite diverse, the value and norm development step allows the organization to adopt a new set of cultural values and norms that will support the adoption of a market orientation. An example of a value includes the "market as the raison d'être" (Gebhardt et al., 2006, p. 43). The behavioral norms that manifests that value are that the decisions and actions of the organization's members always take into consideration the impact on the market. Adoption of a market-oriented cultural value helps the firm transition to the market reconnection step. Successful firms send team members to interview customers and other critical external stakeholder groups. Team representatives then share their insights and experiences, so that all members of the organization can deepen their understanding of the market. The next step in the reconstitution phase involves identifying dissenters. While efforts should be made to encourage their commitment to change, at some point however, dissenters should be removed from the organization and new members—whose philosophy and outlook are more closely aligned with the organization's newly-adopted values—should be recruited. The reconstitution phase culminates with the adoption of a collaborative working strategy, where every task is approached in a "market-oriented manner, precisely because they agree on what the market is, what its unmet needs are, and how to work together to meet those needs" (Gebhardt et al., 2006, p. 46).

Institutionalization—Recognizing the change that has occurred by this point, firms who genuinely desire to adopt a market orientation take steps to formalize these changes. This process entails four distinct steps: formalization, alignment of rewards, indoctrination and training, and power shift. The formalization process is marked by adoption of symbols, rituals, and artifacts that represent the market-oriented culture of the organization. In some cases, this could include changes to the organizational structure. The change is further institutionalized when compensation or other reward systems are tied to the manner in which the organization's members uphold the market-oriented culture. The effort is sustained through the institution of formal training programs for new as well as existing workers. Finally, the organization expands decision-making power to all members of the organization, entrusting them with the authority to make decisions that are in the best interest of the customer.

YanLev/Shutterstock.com

Maintenance—Once an organization has transitioned to an improved market-orientation, research shows that employees begin to reflect on the circumstances that led to the change and who or what was responsible for the successful change. These interpretations tend to differ among employees based on when they joined the organization—before, during, or after the change was adopted. At this point, it becomes important for the organization's leadership to maintain the market-oriented culture. This can occur through rituals that continue to reinforce the organization's values and norms, by implementing on-going market investigations, and focusing on a long-term commitment to the firm's market-oriented culture.

While many schools have been successful in adopting promotional communication strategies to help them become more competitive, fewer have truly transitioned to becoming marketing organizations, whose focus is on identifying customer needs and creating a marketing mix that will result in a successful value exchange.

Chapter 8—Spotlight: Fund-Raising

Due to the financial challenges and funding cuts schools face, many school leaders rely on outside financial assistance from parent teacher organizations or school foundations. In smaller or more rural areas, county-wide community foundations will sometimes have an educational fund-raising arm. Grants from PTA's or School Foundations typically offer support in pre-determined funding categories. These range from music and arts, library resources, professional development, and classroom gifts. Some of the more creative foundations offer student achievement grants, to enable student clubs to participate in state or national competitions. Other novel funding gives matching incentives to teacher proposals posted on donorschoose.org, a donor website where teachers can showcase their grant proposals to receive funding. One suburban Midwest foundation provided $50,000 in matching funds for a state department of education technology grant application made by the district, in order to purchase laptops for the high school.

Schools' fund-raising arms generate donations in a variety of ways. A nonprofit public charter school organization in the Southwest approaches fund-raising in much the same way as private schools, utilizing an Advancement Office and running an annual giving campaign. They report as much as 65% parent participation. In addition to writing grants to public and private funding sources, school foundations use a variety of tactics to raise money, ranging from corporate sponsorship proposals to individual donor foundation memberships. One school foundation reported a drop in individual participation when school registration went paperless. Formerly, paper membership flyers were included with the registration materials, which parents completed and returned with a check. When online registration was instituted, the website included a box for parents to check if they wished to donate to the school foundation, though it is not as successful as the paper appeal. As a result, foundation officers have moved toward setting up tables at the back-to-school nights at each of the district's schools, in order to make a personal appeal to parents.

Foundations also utilize events such as silent auctions or 5k run/walks to realize their fund-raising goals. One school foundation reports that as much of 50% of their annual budget comes from revenue generated through special events. However, with the amount of time, planning, and money that goes into planning an event, some foundation administrators worry about relying too heavily on this form of fund-raising, should weather or other unforeseen circumstances result in an event's cancellation.

Beyond fund-raising, educational foundations are moving into advocacy efforts. Foundation board members are using their positions to advocate for increases in the state funding formulas. Other Foundation board members are using their position to lobby School Board members, in an attempt to influence district spending cuts and other operational matters. Foundations provide an additional arm for schools to engage in deepening their relationships with parents and other community stakeholder groups.

Questions

1. Some critics of private foundation funding for public education point to the disparity that exists between individuals who live in the inner-city versus the wealthy suburbs. Other opponents state that private fund-raising for public education only masks the problem that public education is inadequately funded. What are some of the ethical considerations related to working with or benefitting from an educational foundation? Should private resources be more equitably distributed between schools and districts?
2. Many school foundations seek to engage parents in activities besides fund-raising. What should come first: general engagement and then fund-raising? Or fund-raising and then deepened engagement? What are ways district-wide foundations can increase parent involvement?
3. School foundations often face push-back from parents who do not want to support a district foundation, but would rather have their contribution go directly to their child's school. How can foundations counter this argument?
4. PTA's and foundations can pay for extras. However, the real funding problem for schools is rooted in finding money for teachers. Unfortunately, private sources cannot guarantee sustained funding, and cannot be used for these purposes. How can external funders help solve this problem?

Applying the Concepts

1. Identify a marketing communication activity your school has recently undertaken. What were the goals for the activity? How were they assessed? What was the ROI?
2. Assess your school's current use of social media. Does your school (or district) have a social media policy? Is that policy being followed? How is social media use monitored? Is your school using social media to simply inform the audience or to truly engage the audience? Based on your assessment, what changes would you suggest?

References

Chapman, D. (2012). Tactics to boost social media results. *Franchising World, 44*(11), 15–16.

Farris, P. W., Bendle, N., Pfiefer, P., and Reibstein, D. (2006). *Marketing Metrics: 50+ Metrics Every Executive Should Master.* Upper Saddle River, NJ: Pearson Education, Inc.

Gebhardt, G. F., Carpenter, G. S., and Sherry, J. F. (2006). "Creating a Market Orientation: A Longitudinal, Multifirm, Grounded Analysis of Cultural Transformation." *Journal of Marketing, 70*(4): 37–55.

Gebhardt, G., Carpenter, G., and Sherry, Jr., J. (2009). Creating a market orientation. *KelloggInsight,* April 1. Retrieved January 15, 2014, from: http://insight.kellogg.northwestern.edu/article/walking_the_walk/

Mindruta, R. (2013). Top 10 Free Social Media Monitoring Tools. Retrieved December 18, 2013, from: http://www.brandwatch.com/2013/08/top-10-free-social-media-monitoring-tools/

Norman, C. (2009). 50 Social Media Tactics for Nonprofits. Retrieved December 12, 2013, from: http://amaconnect.marketingpower.com/marketing_sector/nonprofit_marketing/m/nonprofit_marketing_file_gallery/3803.aspx

Social Media Governance. Retrieved December 18, 2013, from: http://socialmediagovernance.com/policies.

Stelzner, M. (2013). *Social Media Marketing Industry Report: How Marketers Are Using Social Media to Grow Their Businesses*. Retrieved December 2, 2013, from: http://www.socialmediaexaminer.com/report/.

Whalen, D., & Krishna, S. (2013). The double-edged sword of social media. *NASD Directorship 39*(5). 68.

Chapter 9

From Lesson Plans to Marketing Plans

We see our customers as invited guests to a party, and we are the hosts. It's our job every day to make every important aspect of the customer experience a little bit better.

—Jeff Bezos, Founder of Amazon.com

Comprehensive lesson plans are a critical part of good education. As a teacher you must be able to write and implement lesson plans. As a school leader you must be able to review lesson plans and provide teachers support in their lesson planning. Crafting a successful marketing plan is just as important. The following tools will help educators through each stage of the marketing planning process.

Position Statement Development

Value Exchange

Define the value you provide the community: _____

_____

_____

_____

_____

_____

_____

Complete the Perception Map

Value Exchange
Status Quo

Indicator

Value
Exchange

Public School **The Seller**

Family **The Buyer**

Positioning Statement: _____

_____

_____

_____

_____

_____

_____

Bildagentur Zoonar GmbH

Market Research Checklist

1. Objective of Research:

_____

_____

2. What sources will you use and what data will you collect?

_____

_____

3. What is your collection timeline and methods for collection?

_____

_____

4. What does your data say and what does it mean for your marketing efforts?

_____

_____

Marketing Plan Template

Product: (What are you trying to promote?)

_____

Target Audience: (To whom are you selling or promoting your product?)

_____

Objective: (What do you want your Target Audience to do?)

_____

Timeline: (How long will your activity last?)

_____

Measurement: (How will you measure the success made toward realizing your objective?)

_____

Marketing Mix Considerations

Product

Does the product (service), as it stands right now, meet the needs of your target customers?
Yes   No

If YES—what need does the product meet? How specifically does the product meet those needs?

If NO—what changes, additions need to occur so that the product meets the needs of your target audience?

Price (Value)

What level of value do the members of our target audience assign to our product?

_____   Tremendous value. Our product is seen as the superior option in all respects. Why?

_____   Some value. Our product is viewed as comparable to other competing options. Why?

_____   Lesser value. Our product is viewed as somewhat less valuable than other completion options. Why?

_____   Limited value. Our product is viewed as offering considerably limited value, relative to competing options. Why?

If my value proposition is not what I hope it could be, what changes do I need to make to the product to increase the value proposition?

If my value proposition is excellent, what changes do I need to make to the other aspects of my marketing mix?

Place

Do the members of my target have easy and open access to my product?   Yes   No

If NO, what are 3–5 things we could do to improve access to the product?

Would making changes to the access to my product also allow me to reach new customers? Why? How?

What barriers or challenges must be overcome in order to improve access? Explain.

Promotion

How has this organization typically promoted this (or a similar) product?

Should anything from the existing, traditional strategy be dropped? Why?

What new promotional tools or strategies should we try which will help us promote this product? Why?

Marketing Budget Tracking Sheet

Expense Category	Jul	Aug	Sept	Oct	Nov	Dec	Jan	Feb	Mar	Apr	May	Jun	Total
Marketing Research													
Primary research													
Secondary research													
Databases/licenses													
Mktg Research Total													$
Marketing Communication													
Advertising													
Public Relations													
Direct Mktg.													
Events													
Sales Promotion													
Website/social media													
Printing													
Other													
Mktg Comm Total													$
Student Acquisition & Retention													
Lead generation													
Student retention													
Acq./Ret. Total													$
Other													
Postage													
Travel													
Other													
Other Total													$
Total Mktg Budget													$

Andresr/Shutterstock.com

Marketing Plan Implementation Tracking Sheet

In order to achieve our objective, what items need to occur?

- ► First brainstorm for *all* of the items or tasks that need to happen
- ► Review the list and then try to put them in a sequential order
- ► Identify the person/department/function that is either responsible for the task or is involved in some way

Task	Time Frame	Responsible Party

CPSIA information can be obtained at www.ICGtesting.com
Printed in the USA
LVOW03s0617290415

436288LV00001B/1/P